I0804322

IMAGES
of America

SAN LUIS OBISPO COUNTY SHERIFF'S DEPARTMENT

On the Cover: Sheriff Yancy McFadden rides a horse during a parade along Park Street in downtown Paso Robles in 1909. A sterling silver sheriff badge is visible on his jacket. According to the custom of the days before the use of uniforms, badges were displayed upon the outermost garment for identification. (Gary Hoving collection.)

IMAGES
of America

SAN LUIS OBISPO COUNTY SHERIFF'S DEPARTMENT

Gary L. Hoving

ARCADIA
PUBLISHING

ISBN 978-0-7385-7545-2

Published by Arcadia Publishing
Charleston, South Carolina

Printed in the United States of America

Library of Congress Control Number: 2011920140

For all general information, please contact Arcadia Publishing:
Telephone 843-853-2070
Fax 843-853-0044
E-mail sales@arcadiapublishing.com
For customer service and orders:
Toll-Free 1-888-313-2665

Visit us on the Internet at www.arcadiapublishing.com

This historical portrayal is dedicated to the members of the San Luis Obispo County Sheriff's Department, past and present, who have worked diligently for the safety of the community.

Contents

Acknowledgments 6

Introduction 7

1. The Birth of a County 9
2. The Century Turns 19
3. War and Postwar Law Enforcement 31
4. Progressing into the Modern Era 61
5. A Promising Future 123

The California Law Enforcement Historical Society 127

ACKNOWLEDGMENTS

The creation of any book requires a great deal of time from the author and those who assist in its preparation. This book is certainly no different. My grateful appreciation is extended to the editorial team, proofreaders, and photograph identifiers. My thanks go to all of those who assisted in this production, including Crystal Hoving, Beatrice Hodges, Debra Holman, Anthony Wood, Mark Pytko, Linda Austin, Jill Hoving, and Russell Flores. Additionally, my appreciation goes to the San Luis Obispo County Sheriff's Department, which authorized the use of modern photographs approved by Sheriff Patrick Hedges. All official sheriff's department photographs are acknowledged as "SLOSD" after each use.

A special note of thanks is extended to the family of Mary Waterbury. Mary was the victim of a murder whose case remained undetected for 19 years until justice was administered. In an odd twist of fate, a family predecessor of Mary Waterbury was a deputy sheriff in San Luis Obispo County, and a photograph from the family collection has been included.

I would like to thank my family for their patience and support during the development of this project. Our children—Stephanie Codding, Jill Hoving, Carly To, and Stephanie Hranek—continue to be a great inspiration.

Unless otherwise noted, all images are part of the author's collection.

INTRODUCTION

San Luis Obispo County is located between Los Angeles and San Francisco along the beautiful central coast of California. Sprawling over 3,300 square miles, the large geographic area remains small in overall population at nearly 270,000. Like many areas in the state, San Luis Obispo was originally established by Catholic missionaries who built a chain of churches. These missions served to settle the state and lead native peoples to Catholicism. California missions often served as the roots for communities that grew around them.

In the early days, with an absence of roadways or railways, San Luis Obispo was primarily serviced by traders aboard ships docking at Port Harford. Not until 1894 was rail access completed into the county, which permitted supplies to reach the area in greater quantities. This isolation required residents to be primarily self-sufficient in growing and raising items needed to sustain their existence. Even today, agriculture is the number one commodity in the county. However, the cattle industry has now fallen behind the wine crop as the largest cash producer.

With the train connection being dedicated on May 5, 1894, San Luis Obispo was able to link passengers and other goods with the metropolitan centers of California. The Southern Pacific rail access had a profound impact on the growth of the county, which had remained rather secluded from the rest of the state.

Prior to about 1900, San Luis Obispo County was notorious for the high numbers of outlaws and highwaymen hidden in the hills surrounding the community. Holdups of travelers on horseback and in stagecoaches were much more commonplace than anyone would suspect from such a serene setting. From the very beginning of the county, lawlessness was commonplace. An example would be the murder of nine people at Mission San Miguel in October 1849. A band of American sailors made their way into the small mission in northern San Luis Obispo County, killing all there, including an infant. A posse was formed, and all of the killers were located along trails between San Luis Obispo and Carpenteria, in southern Santa Barbara County. One by one, the offenders were shot dead by the posse members, who swiftly administered justice in the fashion of the true Old West.

Electing a sheriff to protect a county of such great size was ineffective and extremely risky. The first sheriff, Henry Dalley, considered the job so dangerous that he resigned prior to the completion of his first term in office. Sheriffs did, however, have the authority to deputize as many men as necessary to get the job done. These early deputy sheriffs were of good character, but they received no training and were unpaid for their service.

Another type of law enforcement officer was available to help the sheriff maintain the peace. Each judicial township elected a constable, who would serve civil papers and arrest warrants at the discretion of the court. These constables and their deputies were not paid a salary but received a fee for each day they served in the courtroom and every process they served. While certainly not frontline law enforcers, they were frequently pressed into service in aid of the sheriff and his deputies.

With 161 years of history, the San Luis Obispo County Sheriff's Department has seen many changes in the delivery of service. Perhaps the biggest impact is in the speed of communications.

To summon the service of the sheriff, citizens would originally send messengers from anywhere in San Luis Obispo County on horseback. Upon reaching the county seat, the messengers would locate the sheriff and describe the problem and location. The sheriff would either respond by horseback immediately or assemble a posse and head out toward the emergency. Unfortunately, this response could take several days to reach an outlying community.

Improvements such as telegraphs and telephones began to cut the response time by allowing the sheriff to be notified much earlier. The telegraph was used commercially as early as 1843, but it was not for another 50 years that it became available in San Luis Obispo. Even then, the lines reached San Luis Obispo, but they did not extend to all of the communities.

Adoption of a radio system for law enforcement in San Luis Obispo started in the mid-1940s as the two-way radio systems began to improve primarily based on wartime needs. A direct radio link between sheriff's headquarters and patrol cars drastically reduced the amount of time needed to respond to a call for service. Of course, by this time, deputies were driving vehicles, which was probably a greater time-saver than the radio when compared to horseback response.

Today, a trial program of in-car computers link directly to the communications center, which eliminates any delay in broadcasting calls. This enhanced communication system is capable of sending photographs, maps, directions, and even fingerprints to field personnel.

Training enhancements have clearly aided in the quality of service delivered to the community. Mandated core training classes and continuing education have raised the performance of department employees significantly. Although no deputies had any academy training until 1963, all sworn personnel now undergo an extensive basic academy training program followed by a field-training program. It is nearly one year until a deputy is released to the field as a solo officer.

The manner of training has also evolved over the years. Initially, all courses were delivered in person from an instructor in a traditional classroom setting. Now, training sessions in live, Internet-connected courses permit one instructor to deliver classes to hundreds of students at their computers anywhere in the state. Other online interactive training programs provide continuing advanced officer training without the expense of traveling for students.

Finally, weapons have seen a significant change since 1850. Early sheriffs would use any type of weapon that they happened to own. At that point, the cap-and-ball pistol or rifle was in use, followed by the center-fire cartridge. From loading one round, firing, and then reloading to high capacity ammunition magazines and night-vision attachments, each improvement was significant. The greatest impact, however, was the availability of a variety of weapons systems dependent upon the nature of a situation.

Nonlethal and less lethal options of force have changed how field enforcement is delivered. In the early 1970s, the widespread use of a chemical aerosol spray, Mace, was a turning point in force options. From that point, deputies could choose a chemical to control a situation that once could only be met with either a firearm or an impact strike. Currently, patrol cars are equipped with less lethal, beanbag-shooting shotguns and nonlethal PepperBall guns, which shoot small, paintball-sized capsules containing pepper powder. Tasers that administer high-voltage current are also available, creating a safer option for the arrestee and personnel.

Changes in technologies, tools and training have advanced remarkably during the past 160 years, and the future promises even greater improvements. With the evolution of electronic data systems, the working environment for the deputy sheriff of the future is truly unimaginable.

From horseback to gigabit, the San Luis Obispo County Sheriff's Department has been serving the community with pride since 1850. Challenges and obstacles are certain to appear in the future, but the resourcefulness and dedication of the staff will guarantee continuing service of the highest standard.

One

The Birth of a County

The area known as San Luis Obispo was originally inhabited by Native Americans later known as the Chumash Indians. It then fell under Mexican rule and was protected by the office of *juez de paz*, or justice of the peace, which was created on March 20, 1837. In 1846, protection responsibilities were assumed by the office of *alcalde*, which was a term used for general government as well.

San Luis Obispo County was formally created by legislative act on February 18, 1850, becoming one of California's original 27 counties. The legislators chose not to become a territory of the United States but to quickly become a state. California was accepted into the union of the United States on September 9, 1850. The county covered about 3,284 square miles measuring approximately 90 miles long and 64 miles wide. The population in 1850 was 336, consisting mainly of landowners and their employees on large ranches, with over 500,000 acres.

The office of sheriff was created as dictated by California's state constitution, and prominent rancher Henry Dalley was elected to that position in April 1850. Space for his office, a jail, and a courtroom was established inside Mission San Luis Obispo de Tolosa, which had been the center of the region since being established in 1772. Salary for the sheriff was established at $20 per month plus S6 per day for attending the court of sessions. He was also authorized to appoint a jailer at a salary of $25 per month and was allowed $36 per month for the care of each prisoner.

Sheriff Dalley did not complete his elected term as sheriff. In that era, the mountains surrounding San Luis Obispo were filled with more than their share of highway robbers, and lawlessness was commonplace.

The office of sheriff is mandated by the Constitution of the State of California. Each county must maintain a sheriff who is elected as the chief law enforcement officer. Originally elected for a two-year term, the limit has now been extended to four years.

Upon the acceptance of California into the United States on September 9, 1850, the first sheriff's office, courtroom, and jail were established inside Mission San Luis Obispo de Tolosa. Henry Dalley was elected as the first sheriff. He was also a skilled carpenter and built benches for the courtroom. Dalley resigned his office prior to the expiration of his term due to the dangers of the job.

The need for a permanent and secure jail was recognized by the county board of supervisors, who budgeted $13,500 to build a brick-and-stone jail at the corner of Santa Rosa and Palm Streets. With 13-foot-tall walls, the jail contained six interior jail cells, one confinement room, one jailer's quarters, and a water closet. The jail accepted its first guests in 1861.

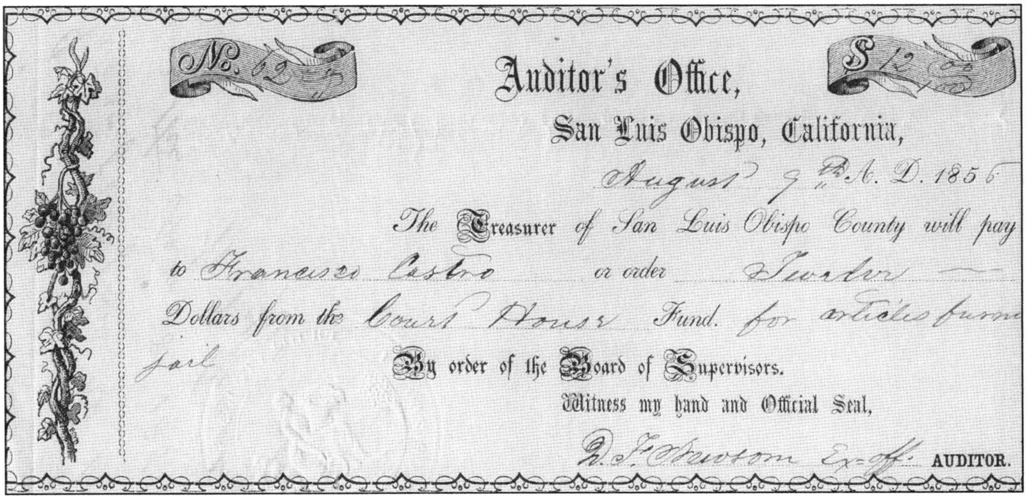

No. 62

Auditor's Office,

$12 00/100

San Luis Obispo, California,

August 9th A. D. 1856

The Treasurer of San Luis Obispo County will pay to Francisco Castro or order Twelve — Dollars from the Court House Fund. for articles furn[illegible] jail

By order of the Board of Supervisors.

Witness my hand and Official Seal,

D. F. Newsom Ex-off. AUDITOR.

A check issued to Sheriff Francisco Castro in 1856 for articles to furnish the county jail has survived history. David F. Newsome signed the check as ex-officio auditor and actually served full-time as the county clerk. In addition, he had been sworn in as a deputy sheriff, which was not a full-time commission.

Around 1885, the entire staff of the county government poses on the steps of the courthouse and county office building located at the corner of Monterey and Osos Streets in downtown San Luis Obispo. Sheriff McLeod is seated on the top left of the steps holding his hat up with his left hand.

An early view from inside the office of Sheriff McLeod shows some rather sparse accommodations, with a single wooden chair and a bentwood guest chair in 1885. A kerosene lamp sits atop his desk well before the introduction of electricity to the building. McLeod is 58 years old in this image.

The badge worn by Sheriff McLeod in 1885 was actually made of tin with the wording "Sheriff, S.L.O. Cala." It was hand-painted and not made by a professional jeweler, as would be expected. While it is uncertain if this was his usual badge or designed as a campaign identifier, McLeod had been seen wearing the star in another photograph taken upon the completion of the Creston jail.

The stately courthouse located on the corner of Monterey and Osos Streets was the center of county government. The sheriff's office and jail was located on the basement level, with access from the left side of the grand staircase into the building. This structure was completed in May 1873 and served the county until it was replaced in 1940.

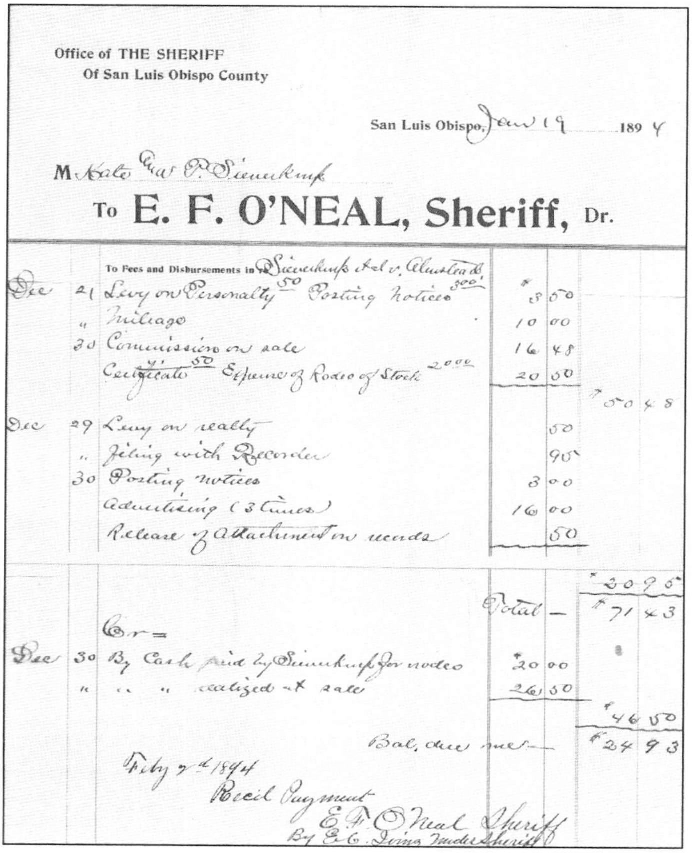

Office of THE SHERIFF
Of San Luis Obispo County

San Luis Obispo, Jan 19 1894

M Kate & W. P. Sieuenkup

To **E. F. O'NEAL, Sheriff,** Dr.

To Fees and Disbursements in Sieuenkup Ad v. Almstead

Dec	21	Levy on Personalty .50 Posting notices 3.00	$3 50		
	"	Mileage	10 00		
	30	Commission on sale	16 48		
		Certificate 1.50 Expense of Rodeo of Stock 20.00	20 50		
					$50 48
Dec	29	Levy on realty		50	
	"	Filing with Recorder		90	
	30	Posting notices	3 00		
		Advertising (3 times)	16 00		
		Release of attachment on records		50	
					$20 90
			Total —		$71 43
		Cr =			
Dec	30	By Cash paid by Sieuenkup for notices	$20 00		
	"	" " realized at sale	26 50		
					$46 50
			Bal. due me —		$24 93

Feby 7th 1894
Recd Payment
E. F. O'Neal Sheriff
By E. C. Ivins Under Sheriff

The ledger prepared by Sheriff O'Neal in 1894 itemized the billable fees for services performed such as placement of a levy, advertising sheriff's sales, and the release of civil attachments. While the sheriff received a small salary from the county, much of his personal income was derived from the retention of service fees. This document was prepared by Undersheriff E.C. Ivins, who was later elected as sheriff.

Jake See was an unsuccessful candidate for sheriff who used this poster to get votes. He resided in the See Canyon area and was related to the famous candy confectioners with the same last name.

A rare interior view of the sheriff's office is shown. Located in the basement of the courthouse, the sheriff's office included gas-operated lighting, a large safe, a spittoon, and a records processing area. Heat for the office was provided by a wood-burning stove with a flue exhausted through a window. The dark door in the background leads to jail cells.

The entire county government staff had increased by 1910 when this image was taken. Staffers pose on the wooden rear steps of the courthouse, with Sheriff Yancy McFadden in the third row, second from the left. Among those also included in this image are the five-member board of supervisors and the elected officers of clerk, tax collector, and coroner.

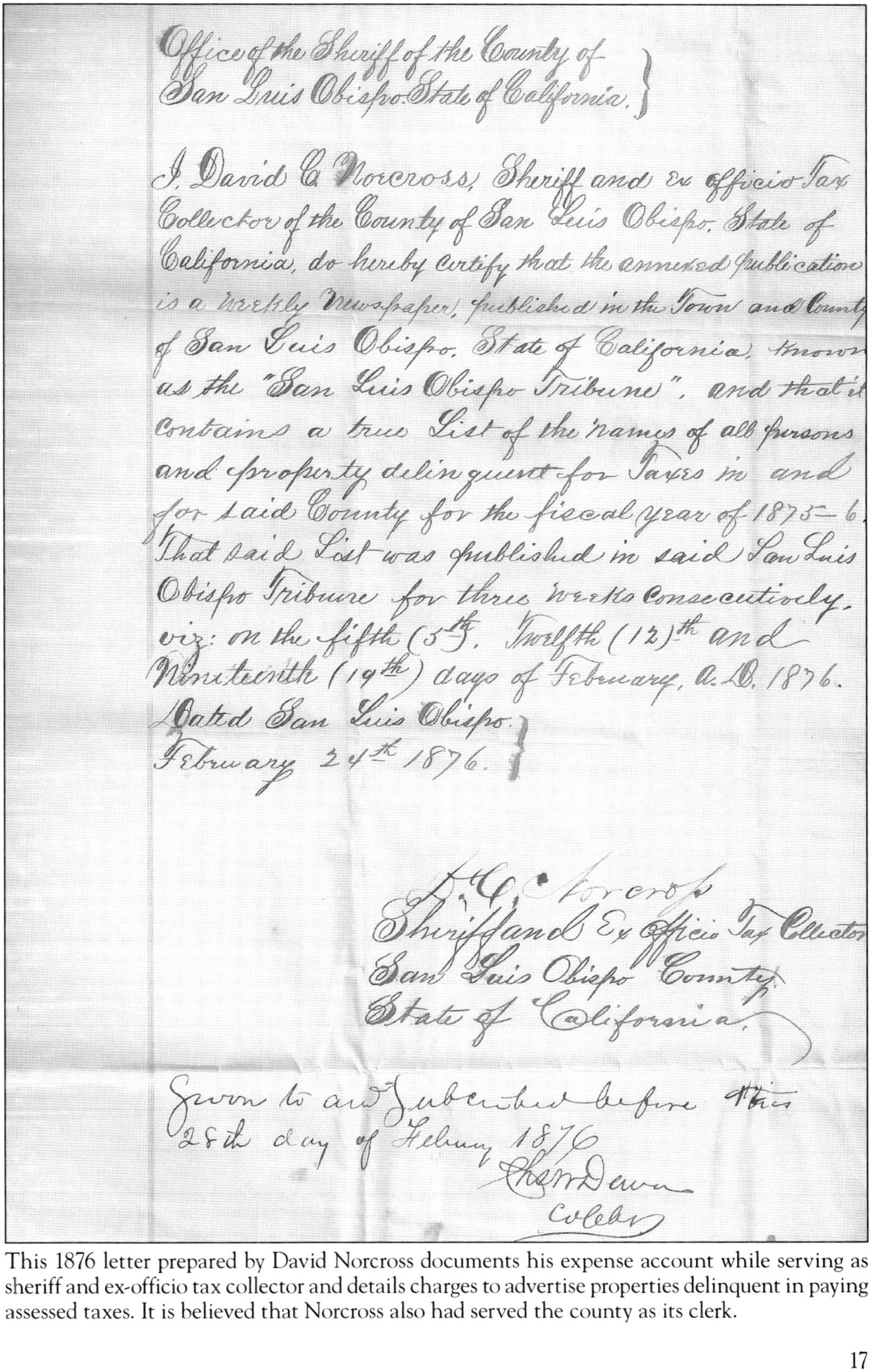

Office of the Sheriff of the County of
San Luis Obispo. State of California.

I, David C. Norcross, Sheriff and ex officio Tax Collector of the County of San Luis Obispo, State of California, do hereby certify that the annexed publication is a weekly Newspaper, published in the Town and County of San Luis Obispo, State of California, known as the "San Luis Obispo Tribune", and that it contains a true List of the names of all persons and property delinquent for Taxes in and for said County for the fiscal year of 1875–6. That said List was published in said San Luis Obispo Tribune for three weeks consecutively, viz: on the fifth (5th), Twelfth (12)th and Nineteenth (19th) days of February, A. D. 1876.

Dated San Luis Obispo.
February 24th 1876.

D. C. Norcross
Sheriff and Ex officio Tax Collector
San Luis Obispo County
State of California.

Sworn to and Subscribed before this
28th day of Febury 1876
Chas W. Dana
Co Clerk

This 1876 letter prepared by David Norcross documents his expense account while serving as sheriff and ex-officio tax collector and details charges to advertise properties delinquent in paying assessed taxes. It is believed that Norcross also had served the county as its clerk.

This is the scene of a 1911 tragedy at the Pacific Coast Railroad crossing at Higuera Street and Portuguese Flat Road that resulted in the filing of criminal charges. The site remains recognizable today under the current name, Elks Lane.

A page from the sheriff's office ledger shows a photograph of an arrestee with a handwritten note indicating his name and that he was a good man but would steal anything. Posting of photographs and identifying information was commonplace in early years. In later years, this was replaced by index cards filed alphabetically.

Two

The Century Turns

Life at turn of the 20th century was changing rapidly even in San Luis Obispo County. Electricity was just becoming available, and the telephone was but a few years away. Train service had been available for only four years.

Transportation would be forever altered with the wide distribution of the automobile in the first 20 years of the century. This would speed the response by the sheriff and his deputies, who had been travelling on foot or by horseback. Of course, the resulting increase in automobiles mandated a set of rules leading to the creation of the California Vehicle Code. Later, that led to a county motorcycle squad that worked from the sheriff's office, patrolling roadways prior to the creation of the California Highway Patrol.

The evolution from the Wild West to a more civilized community was actually slow to arrive in a county of 16,637 residents in 1900. Bandits still roamed the hills, and crime was of concern to many who lived and traveled through the region.

Changes within the sheriff's office became noticeable, as evidenced in some of the images in this chapter. An example would be the abandonment of natural gas lamps in favor of electric lights inside the office. To add electricity to the aging courthouse, wires were strung on the outside of walls to the appropriate lighting fixtures and outlets. While not very attractive, the increased functionality and illumination was welcome.

Communications has always been a challenge to law enforcement throughout the ages. During the early 20th century, before the arrival of the telephone, people would run or ride a horse to the courthouse to summon the sheriff. Information sharing between law enforcement agencies was primarily done through the mail by sending flyers or postcards with information regarding wanted persons. In a dire emergency, the telegraph was used to speed information to other police agencies to aid in the arrest of suspected violators.

While the human resources available to the sheriff were meager, the successes by this small law enforcement agency were very impressive by any standard.

Deputy Sheriff James V. Hogue sports a wood-wheeled bicycle for transportation in 1890. As was the usual custom of the day, a deputy sheriff's badge is pinned to his vest as a form of identification prior to the adoption of a uniform.

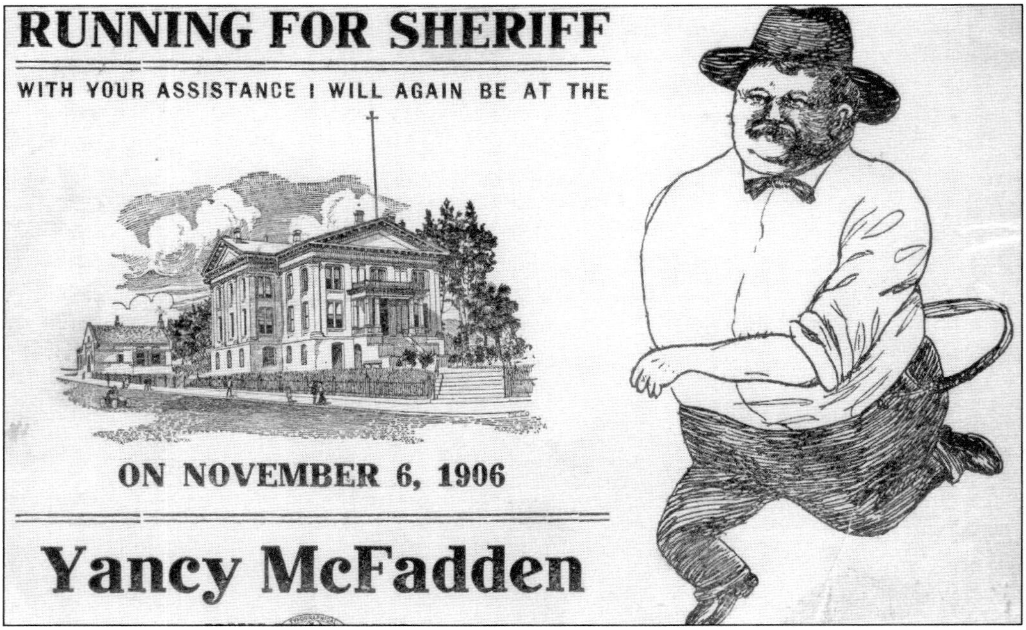

Seeking a second term as sheriff, Yancy McFadden distributed campaign cards with an illustration of the courthouse and a caricature of himself as a very large man. His bid was successful, and he served as sheriff until 1911. The .32-caliber pistol used by Sheriff McFadden was donated by Max Bakke to the California Police Museum in 2008.

The undersheriff's badge worn by Ernest C. Ivins is shown. This is the second-highest position within the sheriff's office. Ivins served in this capacity for his father, Charles, who was the elected sheriff. The senior Ivins suffered from consumption (tuberculosis) and passed away shortly after his term in office had expired.

A father and son from the Simmler family served the community as constable (right) and the justice of the peace. A constable was elected for each judicial township, which could include several separate communities. The justice of the peace served as a judge, although no formal training in the law was required to hold this position.

Escaped---$50 Reward

John Harrison—Escaped from the an Luis Obispo County Jail on the night of June 2, 1910, one of the men who shot Night Watchman John Rude at Paso Robles on the night of March 16, 1910.

JOHN HARRISON,

John Harrison, alias Bert Darrell, alias Bert Ralston, ex-convict Folsom No. 5777: county sent from, Calaveras: crime, burglary: sentence, eight (8) years: nativity, Illinois, weight, 148: size of foot 4 and a half; term, first: age 34: height, 5 feet 7: build, medium: complexion, fair; color of eyes light blue: color of hair: dark brown: date of arrival, Aug. 9, 1904: date of discharge, Dec. 6, 1909; scars and peculiarities, 1 upper front tooth artificial (gold) and fractured: 3 left upper molars gold crowned: 3 dim vaccines left upper arm: dim oblique scar on 3d joint right 3d finger back, dim curved scar 2d finger, right index finger back, dim forked scar at angle of mouth: oval scar right side of back 1 and 1 half inches from median, round scar top of right buttock.

Wanted on 3 charges of assault with attempt to commit murder and burglary.

Please wire at my expense any information in regard to this man to

Y. McFADDEN, Sheriff

San Luis Obispo County, San Luis Obispo, Cal.

A flyer was issued by Sheriff McFadden posting a reward and seeking the arrest of a man who shot the Paso Robles night watchman in an escape from the San Luis Obispo County Jail. Postcards such as this were distributed around the state in order to apprehend a fleeing suspect.

Wanted for Passing Bogus Checks

G. A. Robinson is wanted for passing bogus checks on May 2d, 1908. He is a native American, about 30 or 35 years of age, height about 5 ft. 9 in, and weighs about 150 lbs; light brown hair, smooth shaven, light blue eyes, medium complexion, medium build; plumber and gasfitter; moderate drinker and smokes cigarettes, is a great hand to chew gum: has scar from burn on right jaw bone under ear; one front tooth out of upper jaw on right side; hair light brown, tinted with gray at temples: wore telescope hat, brown suit with stripe about half inch wide running up and down; patent leather low cut shoes nearly new.

Y. McFADDEN,

Sheriff San Luis Obispo County, Cal.

In 1908, Sheriff McFadden sought the arrest a person for passing bogus checks in San Luis Obispo. What is interesting about this postcard-size flyer is the high level of descriptive detail necessary to make positive identification including age, height, weight, hair color, smooth-shaven, light blue eyes, a medium build, and continuing with occupation and social habits that could help locate the suspect.

The entire sheriff's office poses at the basement entrance to the courthouse facility while apparently enjoying a cigar break on September 18, 1904. By this time, electricity had been added to the structure, as evidenced by the wiring above the doorway. Sheriff Charles Ivins is seated in the center of the photograph.

A 1906 overview of San Luis Obispo shows the county courthouse with the hall of records building directly behind. The courthouse is the largest white building on the left side of the image. The remainder of the community is dotted with small homes and a developing downtown commercial area.

The use of deadly force by a peace officer has always been a topic of controversy. In 1918, Constable Frank Bardin was charged with murder for shooting a suspect inside this bar at the Oceano Hotel. He was later charged and tried for murder but was acquitted by a jury, which concluded the death was justifiable homicide.

A second photograph documenting the roadway into, or out of, Oceano was admitted as evidence during the trial against Constable Frank Bardin. The rural setting of Oceano is illustrated by the dirt roads lined with wooden fences. An impressive fact surrounding this incident is that photographic evidence was used during the trial well before forensics became a common discipline.

The 18th Amendment to the Constitution enacted a national Prohibition outlawing the sale of intoxicating alcohol; it was later repealed in 1933. Shown is a large-scale disposal of illegal liquor being poured into the gutter alongside the San Luis Obispo County Courthouse. This photograph was likely used to affirm the local commitment against the use of alcohol. In reality, the law was largely unpopular, and raids as shown here were a rarity.

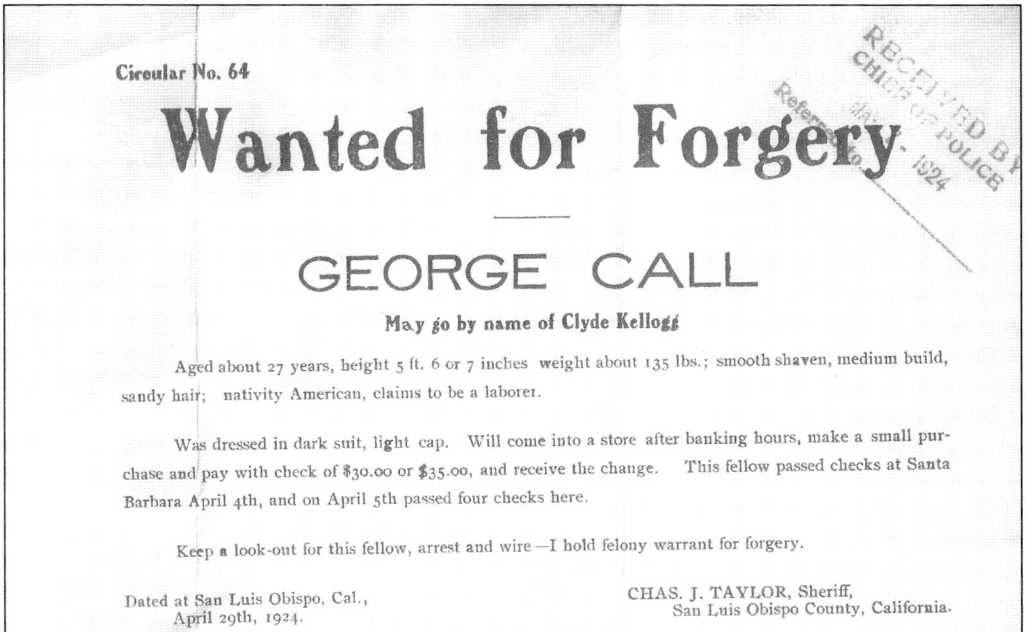

Circular No. 64

Wanted for Forgery

RECEIVED BY CHIEF OF POLICE
Referred to
1924

GEORGE CALL

May go by name of Clyde Kellogg

Aged about 27 years, height 5 ft. 6 or 7 inches weight about 135 lbs.; smooth shaven, medium build, sandy hair; nativity American, claims to be a laborer.

Was dressed in dark suit, light cap. Will come into a store after banking hours, make a small purchase and pay with check of $30.00 or $35.00, and receive the change. This fellow passed checks at Santa Barbara April 4th, and on April 5th passed four checks here.

Keep a look-out for this fellow, arrest and wire—I hold felony warrant for forgery.

Dated at San Luis Obispo, Cal.,
April 29th, 1924.

CHAS. J. TAYLOR, Sheriff,
San Luis Obispo County, California.

Sheriff Charles Taylor distributed a wanted poster for the arrest of a forgery suspect in 1924. By this point, the sheriff would also have had a telephone for communications, but the widespread distribution of postcards was cheaper and took less time. This suspect was also wanted for passing four other forged checks in Santa Barbara in addition to the San Luis Obispo crime.

This 1920 photograph of the sheriff's office interior shows an upgrade to electric lighting, a large collection of record ledgers, wood-burning stove, and the ever-present spittoon. Pictured from left to right are Deputy Hodkins, Sheriff Charles Taylor, Undersheriff Johnson, and Deputy Janes. (Mary Waterbury family collection.)

Charles Taylor was a very popular sheriff and was reelected several times to the office, including the 1918 campaign that used this advertising card. However, his life was cut short in an on-duty traffic accident on the Cuesta Grade while he was driving the only vehicle owned by county government in 1929.

Each arrestee was photographed for identification purposes, including the placement of a mirror that documented the profile. While somewhat uncommon in the 1920s, women were arrested and booked into the county jail, as evidenced here. Close inspection of this group of arrestees leads one to wonder about the reasons for their incarcerations.

Undersheriff Harry Needham stands in the courtyard in front of the sheriff's office in the mid-1930s. Needham had been a career deputy, serving as the second-in-command for several elected sheriffs. Research reveals no indication that he ever sought election to the highest office, even though two sheriffs died while in office during his tenure.

As war escalated in Europe in 1940, America began preparing troops in anticipation of military action. Camp Roberts played a major role in training soldiers, which increased law enforcement activity in San Miguel to the point that a branch jail was constructed that remains near the community park as of 2011.

Arrest for Wife Desertion

Albert F. Mitchell

Nativity American, was born in Pell City, Alabama. Occupation miner, age 22 years, height 5 ft. 6 1-2 in., complexion ruddy, dark hair, blue eyes, smooth shaven, slim face, pointed chin, square shoulders; is an ex-soldier. When he left here on the afternoon of Jan. 20th was wearing blue serge suit, light shirt, blue stripe, white soft collar, lavendar, changeable colored four-in-hand tie with large dots; has blue and red Catholic cross about two inches long on forearm just below elbow joint —think it is on right arm.

This fellow speaks with noticeable southern brogue; was in the Philippines, married a Filipino girl, brought her here, and deserted her. He may rejoin the army in order to make his getaway; look out at the recruiting stations.

Please do what you can in locating this man. Arrest and wire at my expense, I hold felony warrant.

CHAS. J. TAYLOR, Sheriff.

Desertion of a wife constituted a felony in 1921, prompting an arrest warrant and "wanted" flyer by Sheriff Charles Taylor. A felony represents a serious offense and seems extremely harsh by today's standards. Similar behavior—and much worse—committed by a celebrity today receives nothing more than coverage in the tabloids.

SHERIFF'S OFFICE

SAN LUIS OBISPO COUNTY
CALIFORNIA

. TAYLOR
ERIFF

T. J. JANES
UNDER SHERIFF

SAN LUIS OBISPO, CALIFORNIA

ary, I7th, 1923.

In regaard to the Ace motorcycle which I am riding, I wish to state that it now is about fifteen months old and I have rode it about 63,000 miles up to date and it's still shooting fine.

Outside of tires, gas, and oil the upkeep of the machine has cost the County about $II0.00. It has been completely overhauled once and I have ground the valves about eight times.

I have been in this business several years and have rode several different makes of machines but this one has held up better and gave better service than any other one I have ever rode.

Very truly,
George L. Kilbern Captain,
County Motor Police,
San Luis Obispo, Cal.

P.S. Inclose find a couple of pictures of the wheel and myself.

Prior to the creation of the California Highway Patrol on August 14, 1929, most counties operated a traffic squad to enforce the vehicle code. San Luis Obispo had a county motor police led at one time by Capt. George Kilbern, who notes his endorsement of the Ace motorcycle in the above letter.

Three

War and Postwar Law Enforcement

World War II actually started in 1939, and while the United States began preparing for participation, it did not declare war until Hawaii was bombed by the Japanese on December 7, 1941. The county's population in 1940 was 33,246, as Camp Roberts, north of San Miguel, had been actively training soldiers for some time. The influx of soldiers and their families moving near the base resulted in an increase of duties for the tiny sheriff's department. The increase in population was so rapid that the number of deputies rose from three in 1940 to 13 by 1943.

Several other areas were also impacted by the military expansion and training at Camp San Luis Obispo and in Pismo Beach. Pismo Beach was not incorporated at the time, and the patrol of that community was performed by deputy sheriffs.

Aside from dealing with the problems created by off-duty soldiers, San Luis Obispo County was one of the very few homeland locations ever attacked by a foreign government during wartime. The *Montebello*, a Union Oil tanker, was sunk by a Japanese submarine off the coast near Cambria on December 23, 1941.

Deputy sheriffs would patrol in all-black, unmarked sedans during the war years. There was no standardized uniform in that period, and many of the deputies purchased green military uniforms and pinned their badges to their shirts for easy identification. To augment the small number of staff, the sheriff appointed hundreds of "special deputies," honest, reliable citizens who could help the deputies when the need arose. Consequently, hundreds of badges were produced and issued to the auxiliary staff, who served with virtually no training.

Communication was available by calling the sheriff's office by telephone throughout the county to check for service requests. One thing that remained constant was that the best lawmen knew the people of the community who would promptly report suspicious activities. While the term has only been recently applied, "community-based policing" has been in existence since the formation of the sheriff's department.

Sheriff Murray Hathway prevailed in the election against incumbent Sheriff Harry Haskins in 1938. Hathway, a former San Luis Obispo city policeman, continued to be reelected as sheriff until 1955. His first opponent, Harry Haskins, had been the Arroyo Grande postmaster for many years and was the elected constable for Arroyo Grande prior to running for sheriff.

Harry Haskins of Arroyo Grande served one term as sheriff from 1935 to 1939, when he was defeated by Murray C. Hathway. During that era, the entire sheriff's office consisted of the sheriff, an undersheriff, a chief deputy, and one deputy sheriff. The office was augmented by a large number of special deputy sheriffs who served without compensation.

Sheriff Murray Hathway mounts his horse in preparation for a parade through San Luis Obispo in 1950. As an elected official, the sheriff made appearances at many community events to garner support and keep the Old West tradition alive by appearing on horseback. Note the badge worn by Sheriff Hathway is the same one used by Sheriff McFadden in 1909.

This December 24, 1946, photograph includes, from left to right, Lou Whitney, Jack Stevenson, Floyd Crandall, Joe Andre, Pat Davis, Marvin Jatta, Roy Hilton, Sheriff Murray Hathway, Undersheriff Charles Bowden, James Rudsill, Jack Wiley, Albert Call, Sport Raminetti and Meryl McLaury. The badges consisted of a six-point star very similar to the Los Angeles County Sheriff's Department design and possibly influenced by Hathway's good friend Sheriff Eugene Biscailuz, from Los Angeles County.

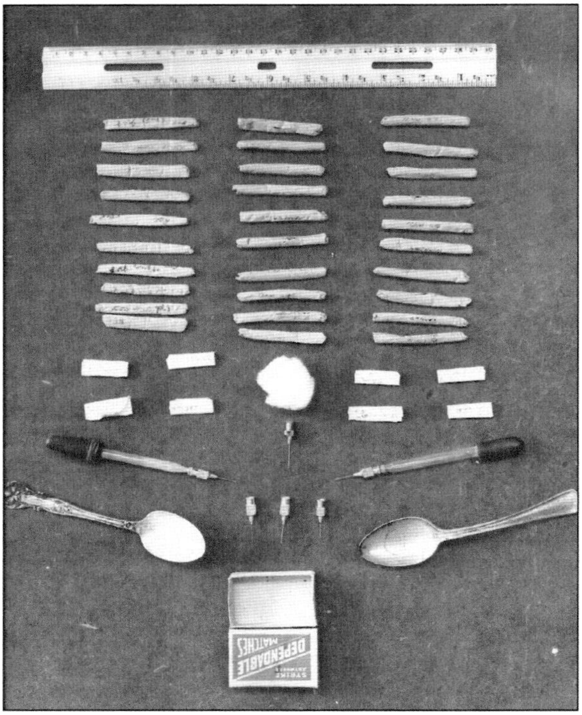

San Luis Obispo County was plagued with drug-related crime as early as the 1950s. Shown here are marijuana cigarettes, bundles of heroin, and crude paraphernalia for injecting drugs—each a felony to possess. Offenders with an illicit holding this large were often sent to prison on the first offense, significantly different from modern sentencing norms.

A pair of marijuana plants was detected in the backyard of an illegal drug fiend, as they were often called, in the 1950s. All drug-related offenses, including possession of marijuana and growing marijuana, warranted separate felony charges with severe penalties. The term medical marijuana had not yet been coined at the time this image was taken.

A young Morley King (first row, far left) is surrounded by investigators during an interrogation at the sheriff's department. From left to right are (first row) Morley King, Sheriff Hathway, and Undersheriff Bowden; (second row) Albert Call, the district attorney, and Deputy Andre. The body of the man's wife had been found murdered and concealed inside a shipping trunk in the basement of a San Luis Obispo hotel.

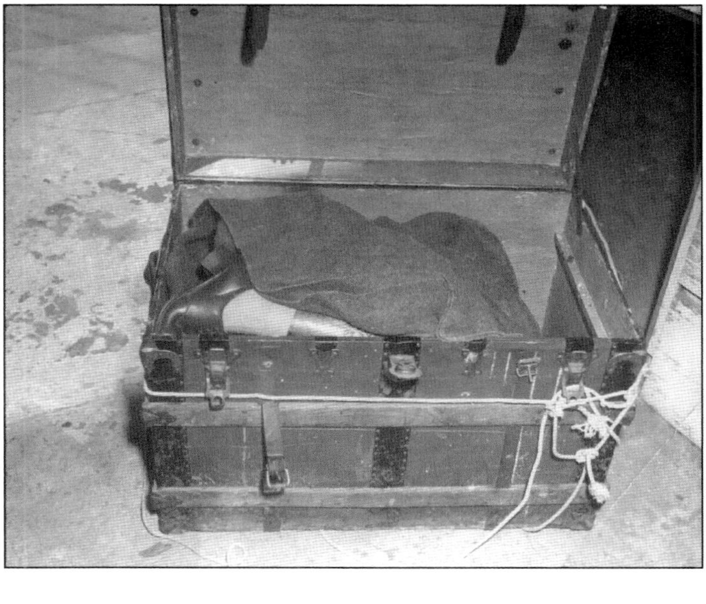

An unusually gruesome murder was discovered in the basement of the Andrews Hotel in downtown San Luis Obispo in 1947. After a lengthy investigation, an arrest warrant was issued for the husband who had fled the area. After he was tracked out of state, a fugitive warrant was issued, and King was placed on the FBI's Ten Most Wanted list. Finally, in 1951, King was arrested in Philadelphia and stood trial for killing his wife.

In the evening prior to June 27, 1952, burglars entered the San Simeon Post Office and grocery store in the remote coastal area of northern San Luis Obispo County. While burglaries were fairly uncommon in that era, the entry into a post office faced a federal offense as well as a state violation when, and if, those involved were captured.

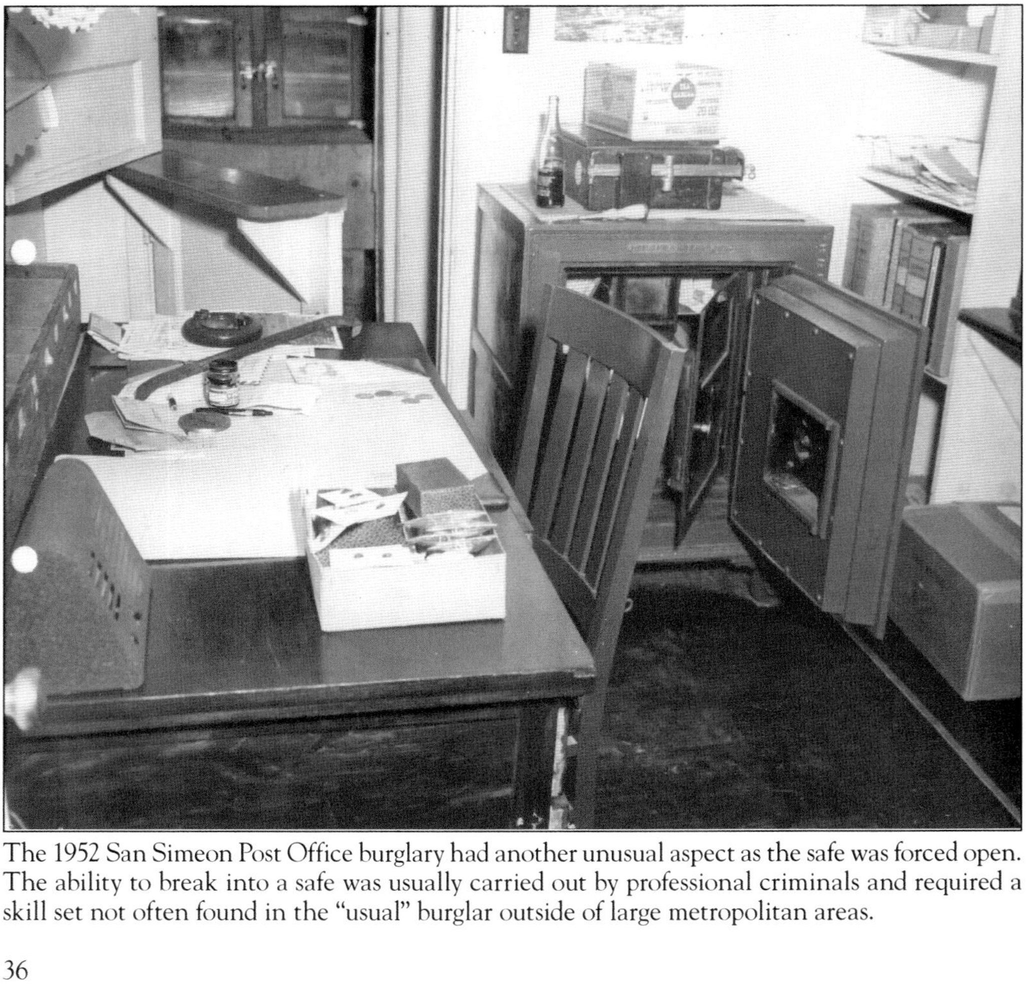

The 1952 San Simeon Post Office burglary had another unusual aspect as the safe was forced open. The ability to break into a safe was usually carried out by professional criminals and required a skill set not often found in the "usual" burglar outside of large metropolitan areas.

Wayne Hillman (center) is escorted to an unmarked detective car by Deputy Charles Bowden (left) and Undersheriff Miles Sander (right) on April 23, 1955. Hillman was transported to San Quentin prison upon conviction of two counts of murder in the shooting death of his wife and her boyfriend at his ranch outside of Paso Robles.

A December 24, 1948, celebration is shown here. Those in the photograph are, from left to right, (first row) Beatrice Johnson, Ann Bowden, Lola Pritchard, and Nora Calvert; (second row) Harold Clogston, Sport Raminetti, Charles Bowden, Sheriff M.C. Hathway, Floyd Hardman, and Floyd Crandall; (third row) Bill Reed, Joe Andre, Jack Stephensen, Maynard Rudesill, Jim Hathway Jr., Ralph Calvert, Jack Able, Chuck Nasland, Harley "Lou" Whitney, B.J. Epperly, and Albert G. Call.

The 1873 courthouse located at Monterey and Osos Street was in need of replacement to modernize and increase the space for county government. Starting in 1936, a new building was constructed in several phases and completed in July 1941. Construction in phases allowed for portions of the new building to be used before the old section was demolished. The total cost of the facility was $416,000.

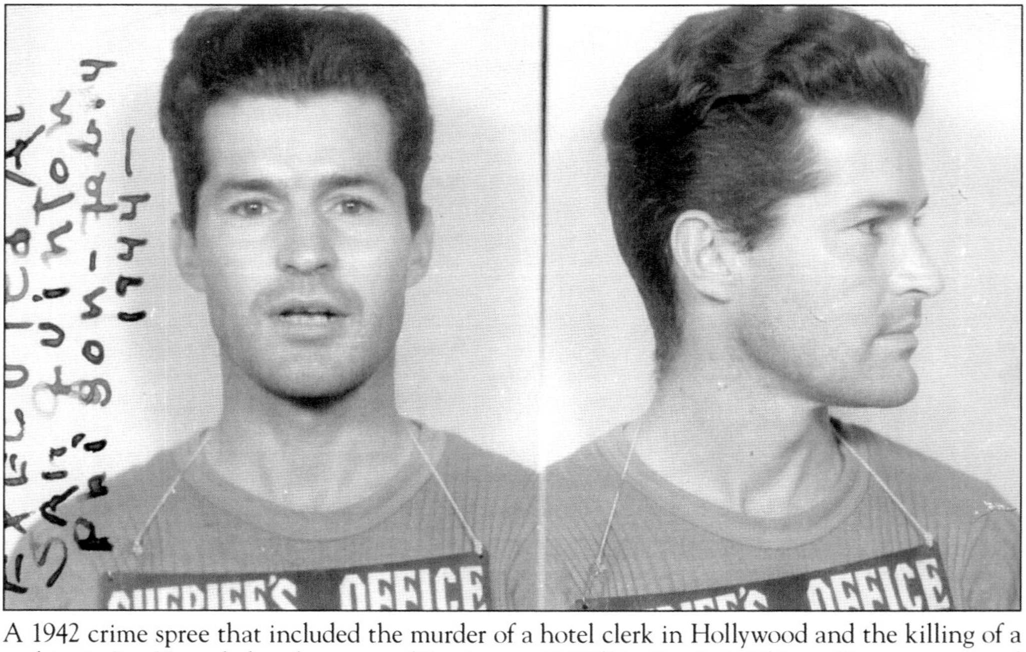

A 1942 crime spree that included the murder of a hotel clerk in Hollywood and the killing of a cashier in Las Vegas led to the arrest of Farrington G. Hill in San Luis Obispo. He was convicted of first-degree murder and executed in the San Quentin gas chamber in 1944.

Sheriff Murray Hathway was assaulted on December 10, 1944, while transporting two fugitives back to San Luis Obispo County onboard a train. Gene Goad and William Crump both made their short-lived escape and were recaptured by Constable Lloyd Skeels. A cut is visible on the temple of Sheriff Hathway as he places handcuffs on prisoner Goad. The incident meant an end to transportation of prisoners by train and a switch to the automobile. Shown from left to right are Sheriff Hathway, Gene Goad, Constable Lloyd Skells, and William Crump.

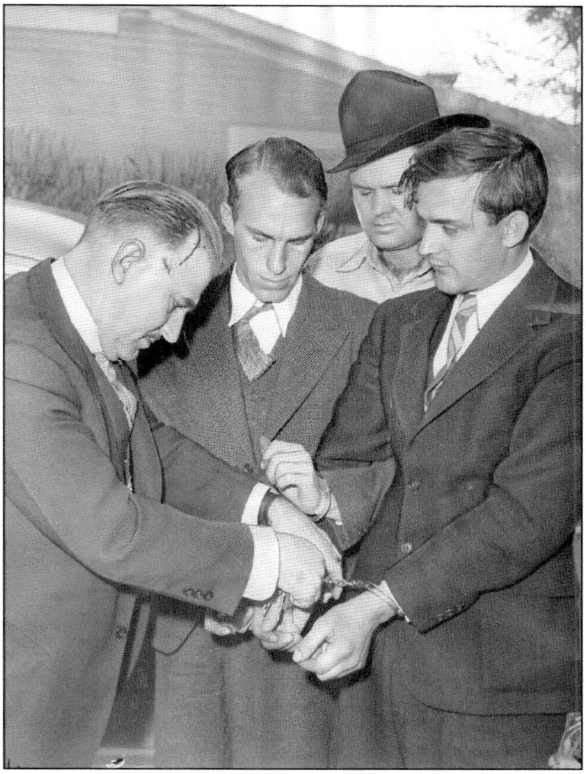

Deputy Sheriff A.Z. "Sport" Raminetti served as the desk officer answering the wall-mounted telephone, transmitting on the radio, and monitoring colored signaling lights indicating that service was needed at specific locations. The wall behind Deputy Raminetti is decorated with licenses to operate a two-way radio, which was a federal mandate through the 1970s.

A frequent visitor to the San Luis Obispo county jail was known as "Badges" (center) for the trinkets he wore on his clothing. He is flanked by Sheriff Murray Hathway (left) and Undersheriff Charles Bowden (right) in the booking area on the fourth floor of the old courthouse around 1953.

Sheriff Murray Hathway (right) pokes fun at a "prisoner" in a fundraising mock jailhouse while wearing his real badge of office and carrying a western handgun. This is the same badge passed on to each successive sheriff elected to office since 1909 until taken out of service by Sheriff L.R. Mansfield in the 1970s.

Upon his retirement, Deputy Kaminetti is presented with a gift by Sheriff Paul Merrick. The impromptu ceremony was conducted in the sheriff's department located on the fourth floor of the courthouse. Note the wall hanging in the background with photographs of each elected sheriff to hold office in San Luis Obispo County.

Paul Merrick ran for sheriff in 1954 and defeated the long-serving Murray Hathway. Merrick had been a deputy sheriff until enlisting in military service when the United States entered World War II. Upon being sworn in as sheriff in January 1955, his office also absorbed the responsibilities of the office of coroner.

Sheriff L. R. Mansfield (center) and the entire staff of 58 employees, including deputy sheriffs, matrons and clerical support, are shown in this 1966 photograph. Mansfield served the citizens of San Luis Obispo as sheriff from 1963 until 1975. He had retired from the California Highway Patrol prior to being elected as sheriff.

A Southern Pacific passenger train derailed and crashed on Cuesta Grande, north of San Luis Obispo on May 10, 1959. Rescue efforts were hampered due to the difficulty of reaching the remote site. These images were captured by Joseph Andre, one of the investigators of the incident.

Two newly appointed deputies pose with their new boss: Deputy Anthony Wood (left), Sheriff L.R. Mansfield (center), and Deputy Sheriff Ismael "Izzy" Flores. Participation in a law enforcement academy was a milestone for the sheriff's department that laid an educational foundation not seen before for the profession. Both men had successful careers, Wood reaching the rank of chief deputy and Flores rising to lieutenant. Flores left in 1979 to become the chief of police in Yuba City.

Deputies Anthony Wood and Izzy Flores stand in formation during graduation ceremonies at the Ventura County Sheriff's Department in 1963. These two young deputies were the first members of the San Luis Obispo Sheriff's Department to attend a law enforcement academy. The academy was held at the sheriff's honor farm in Ojai, where the deputies were housed in barracks.

Under the direction of Sheriff L.R. Mansfield, all uniformed members of the sheriff's department stand in formation for inspection outside the alley entrance to the courthouse in San Luis Obispo in August 1966. This unusual occurrence was covered by KSBY 6, a local television station.

This August 1966 formation included an individual inspection of the rank and file by Sheriff L.R. Mansfield along with his senior staff and guests. Deputies are sporting the newly issued cowboy hat and wearing tan shirts and pants. The cowboy style was not so popular with the line staff, who sought to shed the image of bygone days.

Even non-sworn clerical staff wore uniforms with badges in the 1960s, as seen here. The stylish bow ties were designated solely for female staff members, who were not assigned to field patrol duties. Processing reports in that era was very labor intensive, requiring the use of a typewriter and carbon paper before the use of any type of copying machine.

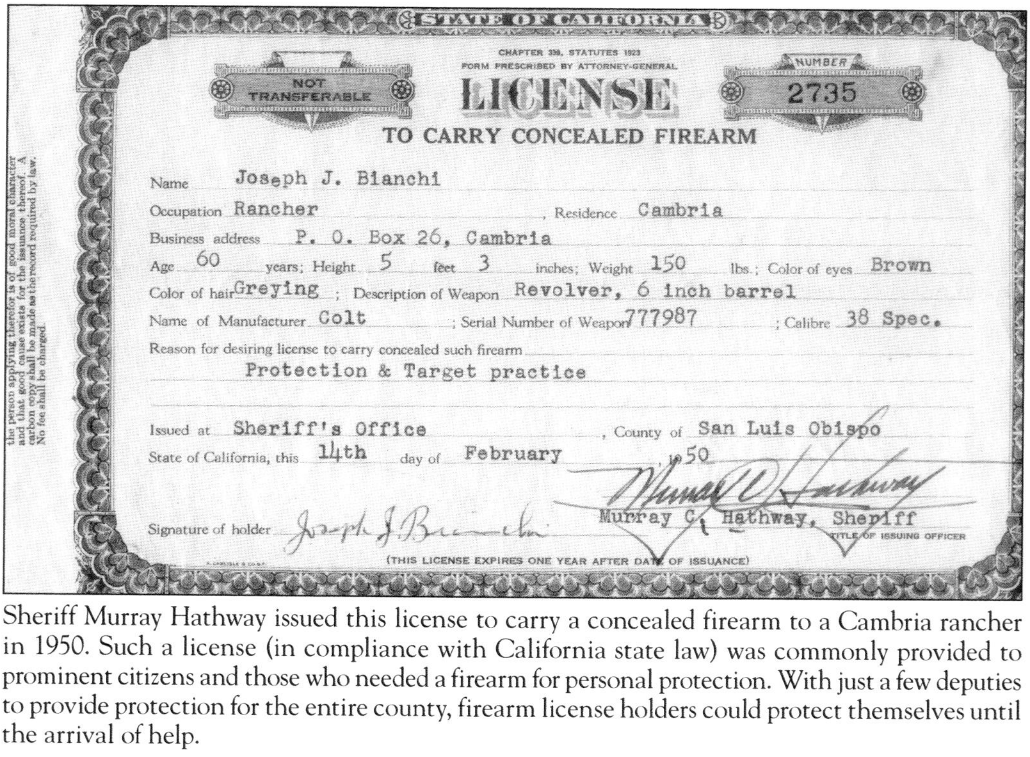

STATE OF CALIFORNIA

CHAPTER 339, STATUTES 1923
FORM PRESCRIBED BY ATTORNEY-GENERAL

NOT TRANSFERABLE

LICENSE

NUMBER 2735

TO CARRY CONCEALED FIREARM

Name Joseph J. Bianchi

Occupation Rancher, Residence Cambria

Business address P. O. Box 26, Cambria

Age 60 years; Height 5 feet 3 inches; Weight 150 lbs.; Color of eyes Brown

Color of hair Greying; Description of Weapon Revolver, 6 inch barrel

Name of Manufacturer Colt; Serial Number of Weapon 777987; Calibre 38 Spec.

Reason for desiring license to carry concealed such firearm

Protection & Target practice

Issued at Sheriff's Office, County of San Luis Obispo

State of California, this 14th day of February, 1950

Signature of holder Joseph J. Bianchi

Murray C. Hathway, Sheriff
TITLE OF ISSUING OFFICER

(THIS LICENSE EXPIRES ONE YEAR AFTER DATE OF ISSUANCE)

the person applying therefor is of good moral character and that good cause exists for the issuance thereof. A carbon copy shall be made as the record required by law. No fee shall be charged.

Sheriff Murray Hathway issued this license to carry a concealed firearm to a Cambria rancher in 1950. Such a license (in compliance with California state law) was commonly provided to prominent citizens and those who needed a firearm for personal protection. With just a few deputies to provide protection for the entire county, firearm license holders could protect themselves until the arrival of help.

Sheriff L.R. Mansfield exhibits the gun-belt and holster worn by Sheriff Yancy McFadden on the steps of the San Luis Obispo County History Center. As may be evident, McFadden was a very rotund individual, permitting his original gun-belt to easily wrap around the slender frame of Mansfield with plenty of spare room.

Deputy Sheriff "Pappy" Clogston works at the booking window of the county jail on the top floor of the courthouse. Inmates were booked at this site by documenting personal identification information, description, and charges. After charges were entered, they were led down a hallway and into an assigned jail cell on the same floor.

Members of the Hell's Angels and other outlaw motorcycle groups were greeted with a roadblock covered by shotguns in the 1960s on their way to an unauthorized rally in the Oso Flaco Lake area of the south county. The heavy law enforcement presence was intended to serve as a deterrent to criminal behavior and encourage the group to consider other locations for future events.

Each person attempting to enter the Oso Flaco motorcycle rally was stopped and checked for warrants, and all vehicles were inspected to determine if they were stolen. Outlaw biker gatherings could result in violence by attendees who resided outside of the area, making such investigations extremely difficult to solve.

Sheriff L.R. Mansfield points the direction out of San Luis Obispo County to an unwelcome member of an outlaw motorcycle club in the mid-1960s. Assisting with the action are Deputy Sheriff Danny Nunez (left) and Constable Larry Nunes. Mansfield was known for his hands-on leadership style and brought many improvements to the organization during his tenure as sheriff.

Lt. Joseph Andre (left) and Deputy Albert Call pose during a mandatory annual uniform inspection. Both men worked primarily as detectives and wore civilian attire on most occasions. As part of their investigative duties, both were skilled in photography and the collection of evidence. The pair made outstanding professional partners and were best of friends when not working.

On May 18, 1958, inmates confined in the county jail found a weakness in the construction of their cell. After they pried loose a blocking plate, a hole was revealed, allowing escape by kicking out the drywall from the ceiling of the office below. Bedsheets were then tied together to serve as a rope, completing their unauthorized freedom.

Motorcycle gangs descending upon the coastal communities proved to be a huge burden on local law enforcement in the 1960s. This scene involving Sgt. Marlin Allen occurred when a large number of motorcyclists chose Cayucos for an impromptu weekend retreat filled with excessive liquor consumption and drugs, disturbing the usual tranquility of the small beachfront community.

Construction of a new courthouse on Palm Street is seen from the viewpoint of the sheriff's department on the fourth floor of the courthouse built in 1940. This photograph was taken on November 21, 1963, the day before the assassination of Pres. John F. Kennedy in Dallas, Texas.

Undersheriff Albert Call is served with a facsimile subpoena commemorating his retirement from the sheriff's department and signed by L.R. Mansfield. Holding the opposing end of the subpoena is Dick Jones, the Border Patrol agent-in-charge of the San Luis Obispo office. Call served the sheriff's department from October 16, 1943, until December 31, 1968.

Deputies assemble in front of Mission San Luis Obispo for a brief inspection and ceremony under the command of Sheriff L.R. Mansfield. Shown, from left to right, are Leroy Mosinski, unidentified, Jake Goodman, Wayne Johnson, Lyle Jenkins, unidentified, Jerry Faeth, and Tim Storton.

Sheriff Lawrence "L.R." Mansfield is seated at his desk in the old courthouse prior to moving the sheriff's office to Kansas Avenue, west of San Luis Obispo in 1971. Mansfield served a full career as a traffic officer with the California Highway Patrol before being elected as sheriff, with a term beginning in 1963.

Hazel Johnson was the first female helicopter pilot in the department's Aero Squadron, shown here about 1960. The all-volunteer group has performed a vital service to San Luis Obispo County since early 1948. The squadron was developed from veterans of World War II who returned to the county with experience as military pilots.

Det. Conrad Feierabend was the founder of the sheriff's crime laboratory in 1968. Here he is seen comparing fingerprints using a magnifying glass. A court exhibit standing upright illustrates a shoe print identification from the scene of a crime. Feierabend came to the sheriff's department with prior experience in the Seal Beach and Morro Bay police departments.

Deputy Sheriff: Salary $844-$1026: Graduation from high school or possession of a G.E.D. certificate. Weight in proportion to height, good moral character and no convictions which could have been punishable by imprisonment in a Federal Penitentiary or State prison. Age: 21 to 45 with experience required for those age 36-45.

Submit official County application form to County Personnel Office, 1015 Monterey Street, San Luis Obispo, California, 93401 by May 10, 1974.

An Equal Opportunity Employer

The recruitment effort for deputy sheriffs was achieved primarily through advertising in a local newspaper. While the educational requirements were minimal, so was the salary. A deputy sheriff in 1974 was paid between $844 with merit increases to a maximum of $1,026 per month. Current starting salary is over five times the top step in 1974.

Deputy Sheriff Wayne Fielder (left) and Deputy Sheriff Donald Hines staff the booking area of the county jail around 1970, prior to the move to Kansas Avenue. Both men are sporting the newly adopted shoulder patch design and the seven-point, ball-tipped star. Tracking of inmates was done with the aid of a chalkboard seen in the background.

Members of the sheriff's department are assembled in front of the San Luis Obispo Veterans Memorial Building for this 1963 photograph with the newly elected sheriff, L.R. Mansfield. The issuance of cowboy-style hats was at the direction of Sheriff Mansfield and was abandoned by 1969, when they were replaced with riot helmets.

Sgt. Danny Nunez demonstrates the proper use of the baton during a training session for members of the California Highway Patrol. This training was conducted at the sheriff's shooting range located in See Canyon, south of San Luis Obispo. Nunez was widely known for his professional training and tactical skills.

Deputy sheriffs receive firearms training with revolvers in the 1960s using a human silhouette target. At the time, the department shooting range was located in See Canyon, prior to the Kansas Avenue complex, which included a shooting range in a more convenient location and enhanced environmental considerations.

An unidentified deputy sheriff inspects the scene of a residential fire which claimed the life of the occupant. Since 1955, each deputy sheriff has also held the commission of deputy coroner. While patrol deputies conduct routine coroner investigations, there is a three-person unit of detectives that conducts more complex coroner investigations.

Det. Leroy Mosinski (left) and Det. Bob Hatley were assigned to coroner investigations during the 1960s. The duties of the coroner were assumed by the sheriff's department on January 1, 1955. Coroner investigators determine the method and manner of deaths involving criminal activity or when the person is not under the care of a medical doctor.

A surplus military Jeep served as the first dedicated vehicle for search-and-rescue missions. After each war, the military dispersed much of its equipment, including vehicles and weapons, to civilian law enforcement use. The sheriff's department is still in possession of two Thompson machine guns acquired at the close of World War II, having paid the government $1 for each.

A specially built vehicle was provided to patrol the Oceano dunes. This duty was assumed by the California State Park Rangers in later years. An area one mile south of Pier Avenue in Oceano is actually a county-owned park, further supporting the response vehicle. Management of the county park was consolidated with the state park system through an agreement with the State of California.

A 1957 Chevrolet patrol car was gray with simple stenciling identifying it as a law enforcement vehicle. Red lights were mounted on the roof along with a spotlight for night patrols. By this time, patrol vehicles were equipped with two-way radios that used a large whip antenna as shown here.

The turbulent 1960s found deputies wearing riot-style helmets at all times while on duty in San Luis Obispo County. This 1968 photograph shows Sgt. Norm Epley (driver) and Sgt. Dan Nunez in a solid gray patrol car. A change to the more conventional black-and-white patrol car was made in 1969.

Around 1965, a deputy patrols Lake Nacimiento in the first patrol boat operated by the sheriff's department. The annual patrolling of the lake from Memorial Day through Labor Day weekend has been necessary due to the high volume of visitors and boating accidents. The unidentified deputy was employed seasonally to enforce boating laws.

Prior to 1970, the sheriff's office was accessed from an alleyway behind the courthouse at Monterey and Osos Streets. A neon sign directed visitors down a short flight of stairs to an express elevator to the sheriff's office on the fourth floor, where the offices and county jail were located.

Four

Progressing into the Modern Era

With the opening of a new sheriff's headquarters on Kansas Avenue dedicated in 1971, the San Luis Obispo County Sheriff's Department entered the modern era. Constructed at a cost of $1.2 million, the new building was specially designed to meet the needs of a law enforcement agency and jail, the facility included designated space for all of the operations of the sheriff except for civil enforcement and bailiffs, which remained in the courthouse. The staff quickly outgrew the new complex, requiring the detective division to move into a warehouse next to headquarters.

Radio communications had been employed for at least 15 years by this point, and now the quality of the two-way radios used in patrol cars was vastly superior to earlier units.

Other advances in this era involved training of all deputy sheriffs. The California Commission on Peace Officers' Standards and Training had designated mandatory and continuing education for personnel throughout the state. Those enhanced training requirements also came with a funding reimbursement for the agencies that complied.

Population growth in the county during the next 40 years was tremendous and resulted in a staff increase to four times the 1970 level. Massive recruitment drives were held, with upwards of 200 candidates applying each year. Much of the growth was in the ranks of the correctional staff needed for the ever-expanding jail system.

To meet a changing law enforcement dynamic required by an ever-changing criminal element, the number of specialized units increased, along with the associated high-tech equipment as well as enhanced training. The Special Enforcement Detail (SED) grew to meet the demand, as training for emergency scenarios that planners hope never occur. Other units born or expanded during this era include the bomb task force, an Aero Squadron, search and rescue, underwater search and recovery, sheriff's auxiliary volunteer patrol, a crime laboratory, and a computer forensics unit.

Patrol units filled with students arrested during the disturbance at Arroyo Grande High School wait in line to access the county jail sally port to book their prisoners. Students were booked on a variety of charges including assault, failure to disperse, and engaging in a riot during the January 17, 1972, event prompting a large-scale response to restore the peace on the campus and in the community.

The grounds of the Arroyo Grande High School turned into a riot-like disruption with a series of fistfights and resulted in the arrest of dozens of students on January 17, 1972. Based on the magnitude of the disturbance, the Arroyo Grande Police Department sought assistance from every law enforcement agency in the county to help restore peace.

Deputies stand near the recently acquired 1969 Dodge patrol cars equipped with massive 440 C.I. engines and sporting the new look, a change from all-gray to a black-and-white color scheme. Standing next to the patrol cars on April 21, 1969, are Deputy Sheriff Bill Andrews (left), Lt. Marlin Allen (center), and Capt. Lloyd Duty.

A reserve deputy sheriff academy graduating class from 1969 shows Sgt. Norm Epley on far right and Sheriff L.R. Mansfield on far left. Jackie Nungaray is third from the right and was one of the longest-tenured employees of the sheriff's department upon her retirement. (SLOSD.)

George S. Whiting served as the sheriff of San Luis Obispo County from 1977 to 1987. He was initially appointed by the board of supervisors to fill a vacancy created by the medical retirement of Sheriff Pierce. Whiting then ran for office, beating Timothy Storton, who had been the undersheriff and acting sheriff. (SLOSD.)

The sheriff's headquarters was moved from the courthouse to a specially designed complex on Kansas Avenue next to Camp San Luis Obispo around 1971. The new building housed the sheriff's administrative wing, records and warrants, detectives, a crime laboratory, and the county jail all under one roof. Undersheriff Albert Call played a critical role in the design of the facility prior to his retirement. (SLOSD.)

Opposition to the Diablo Canyon Nuclear Power Plant received national attention with hoards of media from around the country covering demonstrations and the subsequent arrests. To protect the plant, several levels of defense were implemented to arrest protestors who attempted access through the rugged backcountry surrounding the plant. (SLOSD.)

Scores of protestors assembled on the beach in front of the nuclear power plant entrance took on the air of a music festival rather than a concern for public safety. To the credit of the protest organizers, training was offered to the demonstrators on how to passively resist and attempt access to the facility without risk of injury. Very little force was necessary to effect the arrests. (SLOSD.)

Protestors are interviewed by a local radio station prior to their arrest for trespassing at the Diablo Canyon Nuclear Power Plant in 1981. Opposition to nuclear energy has subsided in recent years, though some groups continue their fights against ongoing operations and voice concerns for storage of spent nuclear fuel rods. (SLOSD.)

A large number of protestors arrested during the nuclear power plant demonstrations were mostly peaceful, with a majority receiving misdemeanor charges for trespassing. In 1981, the protests resulted in the arrest of 1,948, which created a huge burden on the relatively small sheriff's department, necessitating the invocation of the statewide mutual-aid system to bring in hundreds of reinforcements. (SLOSD.)

Assigned as an arrest team during the 1981 nuclear power plant demonstration, Deputies Candi Jones, Gary Hoving, and Scott Thompson are prepared for one of their many long shifts at the facility. In a coincidental turn of events, all three were promoted to sergeant on the same day in 1988.

Sheriff George Whiting is barraged by the press corps regarding the number of arrests and response to protests during the 1981 nuclear power plant demonstrations. Nearly every word spoken by the sheriff was recorded and broadcast on radio and television. Christopher Money, the district attorney, is seen on the far right awaiting his opportunity to address the media. (SLOSD.)

Deputies prepare to address any potential threats resulting from protesting migrant farmworkers in the Oso Flaco Valley about 1983. During that time, the workers sought union representation and the increased rights, salaries, and working conditions shared by many other professions. Leading the cause was Caesar Chavez, who had made previous appearances in San Luis Obispo County. (SLOSD.)

A terrible air disaster occurred on August 24, 1984, when a commuter airplane operated by Swift Air collided head-on with a private airplane. The crash resulted in the loss of all 17 persons onboard the two planes, which impacted near Turri Road, east of Los Osos. (SLOSD.)

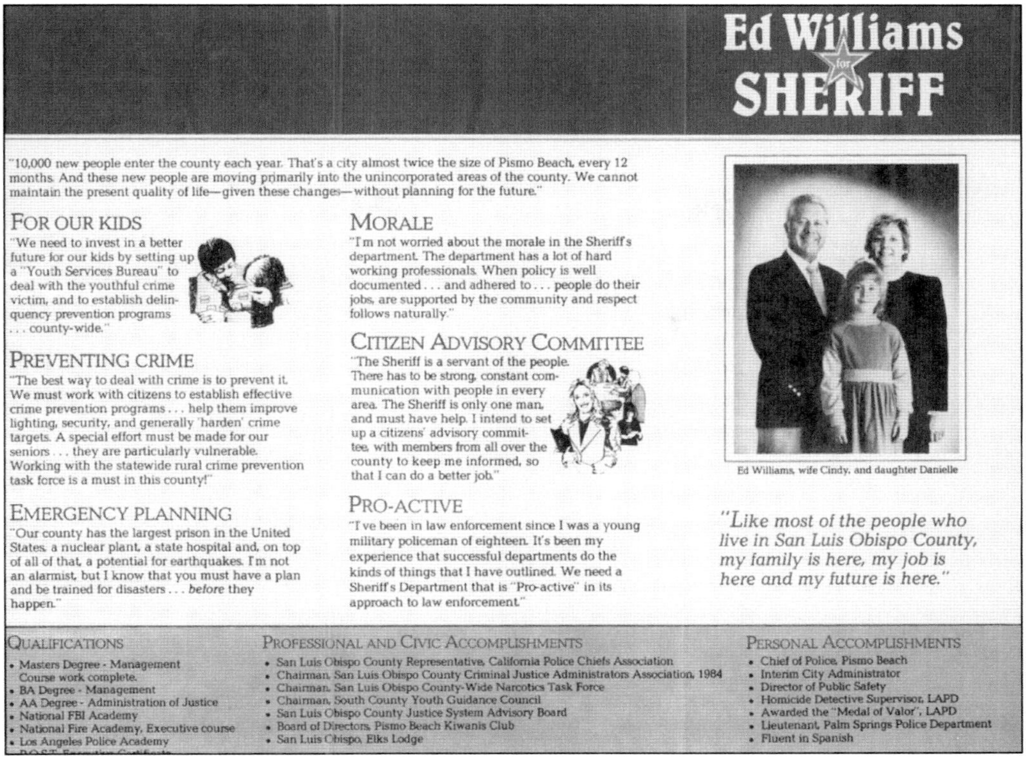

Ed Williams for SHERIFF

"10,000 new people enter the county each year. That's a city almost twice the size of Pismo Beach, every 12 months. And these new people are moving primarily into the unincorporated areas of the county. We cannot maintain the present quality of life—given these changes—without planning for the future."

FOR OUR KIDS

"We need to invest in a better future for our kids by setting up a "Youth Services Bureau" to deal with the youthful crime victim, and to establish delinquency prevention programs . . . county-wide."

PREVENTING CRIME

"The best way to deal with crime is to prevent it. We must work with citizens to establish effective crime prevention programs . . . help them improve lighting, security, and generally 'harden' crime targets. A special effort must be made for our seniors . . . they are particularly vulnerable. Working with the statewide rural crime prevention task force is a must in this county!"

EMERGENCY PLANNING

"Our county has the largest prison in the United States, a nuclear plant, a state hospital and, on top of all of that, a potential for earthquakes. I'm not an alarmist, but I know that you must have a plan and be trained for disasters . . . *before* they happen."

MORALE

"I'm not worried about the morale in the Sheriff's department. The department has a lot of hard working professionals. When policy is well documented . . . and adhered to . . . people do their jobs, are supported by the community and respect follows naturally."

CITIZEN ADVISORY COMMITTEE

"The Sheriff is a servant of the people. There has to be strong, constant communication with people in every area. The Sheriff is only one man, and must have help. I intend to set up a citizens' advisory committee, with members from all over the county to keep me informed, so that I can do a better job."

PRO-ACTIVE

"I've been in law enforcement since I was a young military policeman of eighteen. It's been my experience that successful departments do the kinds of things that I have outlined. We need a Sheriff's Department that is "Pro-active" in its approach to law enforcement."

Ed Williams, wife Cindy, and daughter Danielle

"Like most of the people who live in San Luis Obispo County, my family is here, my job is here and my future is here."

QUALIFICATIONS

- Masters Degree - Management Course work complete.
- BA Degree - Management
- AA Degree - Administration of Justice
- National FBI Academy
- National Fire Academy, Executive course
- Los Angeles Police Academy

PROFESSIONAL AND CIVIC ACCOMPLISHMENTS

- San Luis Obispo County Representative, California Police Chiefs Association
- Chairman, San Luis Obispo County Criminal Justice Administrators Association, 1984
- Chairman, San Luis Obispo County-Wide Narcotics Task Force
- Chairman, South County Youth Guidance Council
- San Luis Obispo County Justice System Advisory Board
- Board of Directors, Pismo Beach Kiwanis Club
- San Luis Obispo, Elks Lodge

PERSONAL ACCOMPLISHMENTS

- Chief of Police, Pismo Beach
- Interim City Administrator
- Director of Public Safety
- Homicide Detective Supervisor, LAPD
- Awarded the "Medal of Valor", LAPD
- Lieutenant, Palm Springs Police Department
- Fluent in Spanish

The year 1986 brought a hotly contested race for sheriff. In a field of six candidates, the primary election reduced the field to the top two vote-getters, Edward Williams and Timothy Storton. At the time, Williams was chief of police in Pismo Beach. He was successful in winning the seat as sheriff, taking office in January 1987.

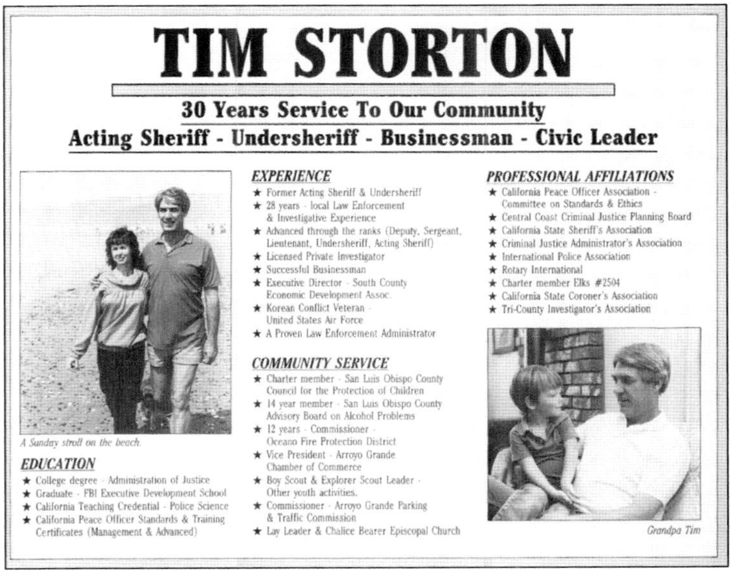

TIM STORTON

30 Years Service To Our Community

Acting Sheriff - Undersheriff - Businessman - Civic Leader

A Sunday stroll on the beach.

EDUCATION

- ★ College degree - Administration of Justice
- ★ Graduate - FBI Executive Development School
- ★ California Teaching Credential - Police Science
- ★ California Peace Officer Standards & Training Certificates (Management & Advanced)

EXPERIENCE

- ★ Former Acting Sheriff & Undersheriff
- ★ 28 years - local Law Enforcement & Investigative Experience
- ★ Advanced through the ranks (Deputy, Sergeant, Lieutenant, Undersheriff, Acting Sheriff)
- ★ Licensed Private Investigator
- ★ Successful Businessman
- ★ Executive Director - South County Economic Development Assoc.
- ★ Korean Conflict Veteran - United States Air Force
- ★ A Proven Law Enforcement Administrator

COMMUNITY SERVICE

- ★ Charter member - San Luis Obispo County Council for the Protection of Children
- ★ 14 year member - San Luis Obispo County Advisory Board on Alcohol Problems
- ★ 12 years - Commissioner - Oceano Fire Protection District
- ★ Vice President - Arroyo Grande Chamber of Commerce
- ★ Boy Scout & Explorer Scout Leader - Other youth activities.
- ★ Commissioner - Arroyo Grande Parking & Traffic Commission
- ★ Lay Leader & Chalice Bearer Episcopal Church

PROFESSIONAL AFFILIATIONS

- ★ California Peace Officer Association - Committee on Standards & Ethics
- ★ Central Coast Criminal Justice Planning Board
- ★ California State Sheriff's Association
- ★ Criminal Justice Administrator's Association
- ★ International Police Association
- ★ Rotary International
- ★ Charter member Elks #2504
- ★ California State Coroner's Association
- ★ Tri-County Investigator's Association

Grandpa Tim

Timothy Storton fought a strong race for sheriff in 1986, after many years of local law enforcement experience and service as acting sheriff and undersheriff. Storton had worked his way through the ranks with the San Luis Obispo County Sheriff's Department after a short tenure with the San Luis Obispo City Police Department.

A large-scale assembly and inspection was held in October 1988 in front of the sheriff's headquarters on Kansas Avenue. Photographed addressing the staff are Chief Deputy Arnie Goble (left) and Sheriff Edward C. Williams. While the logistics for producing such an assembly was a huge challenge, the result was spectacular. (SLOSD.)

A sea of uniformed and civilian staff and volunteers is assembled for an inspection and address by Sheriff Edward C. Williams in 1988. A group of nearly 400 proved to be a very impressive sight, with all groups represented, including sworn personnel, civilian staff, search and rescue, the dive team, the Aero Squadron, and posse. (SLOSD.)

Edward C. Williams was sworn as the sheriff of San Luis Obispo County in 1987. He had an extensive law enforcement career as a sergeant with the Los Angeles Police Department, as a lieutenant with the Palm Springs Police Department, and as chief of police in Pismo Beach. (SLOSD.)

Centered in the photograph during the 1988 inspection is Chief Deputy Tony Wood, who places his hand on Sgt. Gary Hoving. The chief deputy is excusing Hoving's tardiness, as the sergeant had stopped on his way to the inspection to arrest a suspect at a burglary in progress in Oceano. (SLOSD.)

In the 1980s, crowds of tourists flocked to Avila Beach during the summer months requiring deputies to be assigned to the area to control the illegal use of alcohol on the family-friendly beaches. Alternative uniforms were authorized for this desirable assignment as worn by Deputies Larry Davis (left) and Darren Murphy. (SLOSD.)

A successful graffiti abatement program was launched by Sheriff Williams in 1988. Armed with paint donated from a local supplier, inmates from the county jail painted over gang graffiti in an effort to clean up the community. While the above image was taken in Oceano, the program was also conducted in Nipomo. (*Telegram-Tribune*.)

In January 1987, Edward C. Williams (center) accepts the oath of office as sheriff of San Luis Obispo County, administered in the board of supervisors chambers. Williams always maintained a serious and professional demeanor throughout his tenure as sheriff. He also implemented a wide variety of innovative programs and services. (SLOSD.)

Dawn Foster, a long-tenured member of the Sheriff's Aero Squadron, staffs a community education presentation about the services provided by her unit. This particular display was held in conjunction with the grand-opening ceremonies at the sheriff's patrol station in Los Osos. In addition to the static exhibit, a helicopter landed in a field across the street from the station for community members to inspect. (SLOSD.)

Deputies drive over one million miles per year patrolling the streets in San Luis Obispo County. With that many miles, it is inevitable some of the responses might result in traffic accidents such as this rollover near Los Politas. Fortunately, the deputy was not injured in this accident, and the driver's identity remains unknown to history. (SLOSD.)

Deputy Mark Pytko is shown about 1989 with a patrol car displaying a newly coined motto, "Sworn to Serve." The motto resulted from a contest amongst employees, with the Maryleigh Madden-Bost and Carolyn Huseby submitting the winning phrase. Several years later, the words "since 1850" were added to the patrol car logos to honor the department's historical ties to one of California's original counties. (SLOSD.)

Deputy Mark Pytko communicates via radio in a patrol car that is seemingly barren compared to the amount of equipment in current vehicles. Notice the striped cloth attachment on the right epaulet of his uniform shirt, which signifies assignment in the Special Enforcement Detail. The SED is equivalent to the SWAT (special weapons and tactics) teams in other law enforcement agencies. (SLOSD.)

Det. William Bowker reconstructs the pattern of blood spatter during a 1990 crime scene investigation in a rural area near Creston. The investigation resulted in the filing of attempted murder charges against the suspect. As an expert in blood flight characteristics, Bowker was able to determine the position of the victim and the shooter at the moment that shots were fired from this trailer. (SLOSD.)

Commander Larry Davis staffs the sheriff's watch commander's office located in the Emergency Operations Center. During his shift, Davis is responsible for all law enforcement activities in the field for the entire county. In addition, this position plays a critically important role in implementation of emergency procedures surrounding the Diablo Canyon Nuclear Power plant as well as any other type of disaster or emergency situation.

To serve the coastal area, the county established a sheriff's patrol station in Los Osos. A former commercial building was remodeled to meet the needs of the sheriff's deputies assigned to the area. The Coast Station patrols all of the communities from Avila Beach to Ragged Point along California Highway 1. (SLOSD.)

A dedication ceremony was held opening the newly acquired patrol facility in Los Osos. Sheriff Edward Williams spoke about the significance of the station and the impact to the communities served by his staff. Previous coast patrols worked from the headquarters facility on Kansas Avenue in San Luis Obispo. (SLOSD.)

In April 1994, a team of deputies responded to the Los Angeles area to assist in quelling the riots. Briefly posing behind a building burned by rioters are, from left to right, Gary Hoving, Martin Basti, Skip Hebrard, James Taylor, Sean Harvey, Steve Tate, Russ Flores, John Marrs, Keith Scott, Steve Cruce, Steve Himmelrich, Mark Anselmi, Mark Pytko, Nick Fontecchio, Dennis Wizeman, John Giese, and Ben Hall.

A San Luis Obispo County Sheriff's patrol car passes a burned-out commercial business on Normandy Boulevard and Western Avenue in April 1994. Riots broke out in the wake of the acquittal of Los Angeles police officers charged with assaulting Rodney King in Los Angeles. The King incident was videotaped by a citizen and viewed on news channels around the world. (SLOSD.)

San Luis Obispo County deputy sheriffs patrolled the streets of Inglewood during the mutual aid response to the riots spawned by the Rodney King trial. Deputies tend to a victim moments after he was shot in the head. The fleeing suspect was quickly captured by the deputies and arrested for attempted murder. (SLOSD.)

All vehicle stops during the Los Angeles riots were considered high-risk, especially when suspected gang members were involved, which was the case in the above incident. Officers cover the alleged violators while others protect against indirect threats such as drive-by shootings. The San Luis Obispo County Sheriff's Department performed well during this deployment, with no injuries to staff and only one minor traffic accident. (SLOSD.)

Correctional officers Margaret Moore (left) and Bert Reynolds served on the transition team during construction of the expanded county-jail complex and inmate reception center at the Kansas Avenue location. The large project greatly increased housing capacity for male inmates in a design that also boosted officer efficiency. (SLOSD.)

Looking west on Kansas Avenue, the new county jail takes shape, with male housing units, intake and release center, and an expanded sally port that can accommodate more vehicles and large buses with greater ease. The inmate housing area consists of two floors of jail cells serviced by a shared recreational area in a pod formation. (SLOSD.)

A once-in-a-lifetime opportunity was presented by Sheriff Edward Williams, who provided a jailhouse dinner to the public as a fundraiser for the sheriff's volunteer programs prior to opening the facility for inmates. The need for generating additional funding for programs and training was recognized and met with the creation of a Sheriff's Advisory Council. (SLOSD.)

Posed during the jail expansion's grand-opening event are Sgt. Scott Thompson, administrative services officer Karen Colombo, and Capt. Tom Garrity. Garrity and Thompson served as the sworn command staff for the custody division staffed by correctional officers, public officers who serve as professional staff and specialize in the custody of inmates. (SLOSD.)

The sheriff's North County Patrol Station was housed in a rented storefront in a strip mall on Main Street in Templeton prior to the construction of a permanent county-owned building, also in Templeton. Shown in 1991, the original cramped quarters served for a number of years until funding was obtained for a more spacious complex. (SLOSD.)

The Emergency Communications Center is the hub of all enforcement activity operating within the Emergency Operations Center. Accepting 911 calls, dispatching patrol units, directing ambulances, and coordinating all field activities in this 1989 photograph are Jeanne Dague (left) and Kit Rowland. This operation is supported by the sheriff's watch commander, who is located in an adjoining room. (SLOSD.)

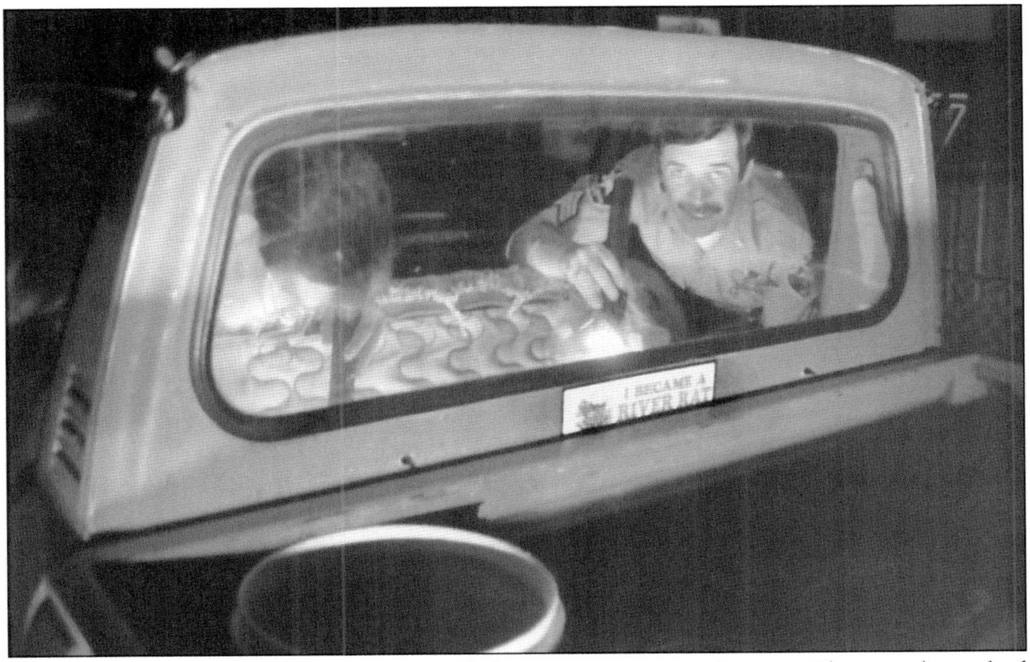

Sgt. Tom Garrity conducts a vehicle search during a car stop in Oceano. This search resulted in the recovery of a shotgun concealed in the truck and led to the arrest of its driver. In the late 1980s, the patrol station was managed by a single sergeant position before creation of the commander rank that is used today. (SLOSD.)

Crime Prevention Specialist Randy Johnson discusses safety techniques during the Sheriff's Citizens' Academy. Participants are receiving instructions prior to operating the FATS (firearms training simulator) system used by sworn personnel to enhance the use of force decision-making and improve shooting skills under pressure. The automated system is surprisingly realistic to students. (SLOSD.)

Prior to the construction of a permanent facility in Oceano, the sheriff's South County Patrol Station was located in modular buildings at the county Regional Center in Arroyo Grande. While the structure was a vast improvement over the previous rented space in Oceano, the Arroyo Grande site was less than ideal for responses to unincorporated areas of the county. (SLOSD.)

Deputies assigned to the South County station pose in front of a sign welcoming visitors to Oceano. Included in the photograph are, from left to right, unidentified, Don Clingman, Bill ? (tow truck driver), Scott Blum, Robert Bullock, James Taylor, Larry Austin, C.J. Bell, Brad Melson, Ken Conway, Tom Garrity, unidentified, unidentified, Henry Stewart, and Colin Clark. (SLOSD.)

A sheriff's explorer program was created around 1998, upon receipt of a start-up grant by the Fraternal Order of Police. Included in the image are, from left to right, unidentified, unidentified, unidentified, Glenn Quackenbush, Jason Rose, unidentified, Jason Maroney, Jill Hoving, and Michael Shipman. An original explorer program was initiated in the 1970s and discontinued by 1975. (SLOSD.)

Deputy Sandy Leber and Lt. Scott Thompson coordinated the sheriff's explorer program shown above in the mid-1990s during a training and social session of future public servants. Standing from left to right are Deputy Sheriff Sandy Leber, unidentified, Mike Shipman, Lt. Scott Thompson, Rebecca Johnson, unidentified, unidentified, and Jill Hoving.

The sheriff's search-and-rescue team converted a former bus into a mobile command center equipped with computers, maps, and radios to oversee operations anywhere in the county. The search-and-rescue team is comprised of dedicated volunteers coordinated by a sheriff's sergeant. (SLOSD.)

One function of the sheriff's search-and-rescue team is to staff the Oceano State Beach Off-Highway Recreational Vehicle area during holiday weekends. After an accident on an all-terrain vehicle, search-and-rescue team members stabilize the patient, extract him from the scene, and place him in a waiting ambulance or medical evacuation helicopter. (SLOSD.)

Deputy Sheriff Doug Scotto and Deputy Sheriff Sonja Ott (O'Donohoe) perform a vehicle stop while on patrol in the south county. After making contact, the deputies await a response from the communication center ensuring that the vehicle is not stolen and that the driver is free from arrest warrants. (SLOSD.)

The growth of the county through the 1980s and 1990s resulted in a greatly expanded level of county service. To accommodate the growing staff, an expanded county government center was added to the existing courthouse and is seen here from the Monterey Street side of the building in San Luis Obispo. (SLOSD.)

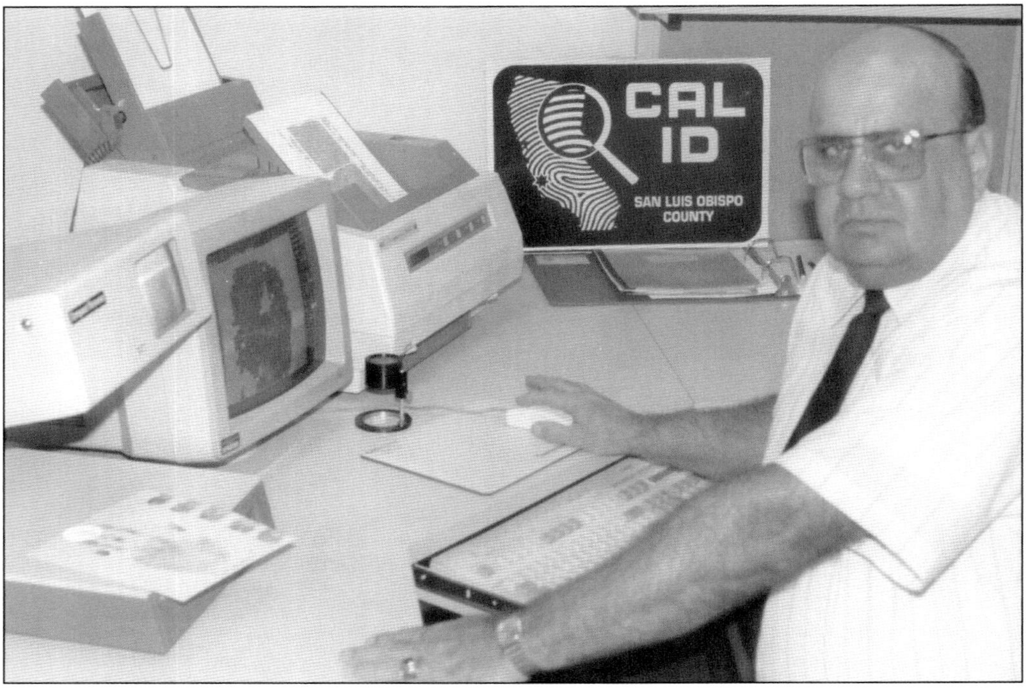

Implementing the first automated fingerprint identification system is James Clark, coordinator of the Cal-ID program in 1989. Clark had previously served with the Arroyo Grande Police Department, working through the ranks and retiring as the chief of police. His managerial expertise developed the program and created the funding source for the countywide operation. (SLOSD.)

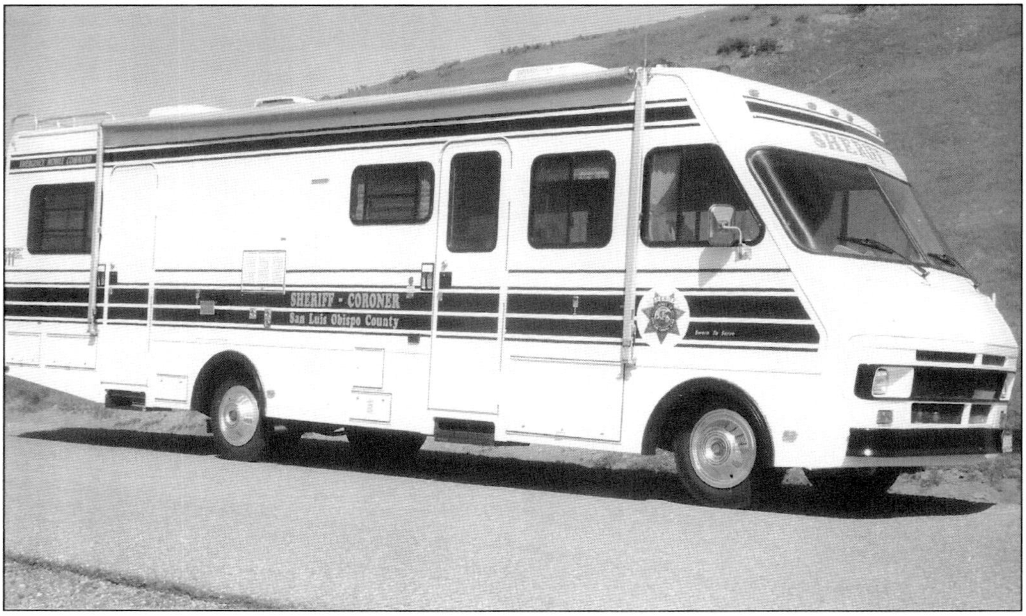

A motor home was purchased and converted to serve as the sheriff's mobile command post around 1990. Outfitted with radios, maps, and copy machines, the vehicle served as a field communications center for command operations during emergencies and is still in use today. The custom paint and letters were applied by inmates from the California Department of Corrections. (SLOSD.)

The official badge of the sheriff's department was changed in 1989 under the direction of Sheriff Williams, who issued a custom-designed seven-point star with the county seal in the center. Many of the previously issued badges used the California State Seal.

Adorned with a black memorial band, the pre-1989 badge issued to the elected sheriff is shown. Memorial bands are worn following the death of an officer or during the National Law Enforcement Memorial Week each May as a tribute to fallen officers.

An aerial view of the sheriff's headquarters complex is shown. The site originally housed only the jail honor farm. The remainder of the operation was occupied upon completion in 1971. The

complex was built in a beautifully majestic setting at the base of Cerro Romualdo, which is a dormant volcano. (SLOSD.)

With a rapid increase in the use of computers in the late 1980s, the sheriff's Automation Unit became a necessity. Shown above are Automation Supervisor Maggie Moore and John Means, who served as an automation technician before promotion to the position of Cal-ID coordinator. The unit has now been expanded to include the computer forensics operation supporting criminal investigations. (SLOSD.)

The staff of the Emergency Operation Center during a major wildfire includes, from left to right, Crime Prevention Specialist Terry Woods, Deputy Skip Hebrard, Lt. Scott Thompson, and Deputy Rich Powell. The emergency operation center serves as a unified command operations and logistics center for any type of emergency or disaster within the county. (SLOSD.)

An award-winning Sheriff's Posse competes during equestrian trials in Southern California. The posse is one of the oldest support units of the sheriff's department and was formed in the early 1940s as the Sheriff's Rangers. The team serves with a parade detail, enforcement unit, and mounted search-and-rescue operation. (SLOSD.)

The Sheriff's Posse is very popular during community exhibitions as shown here. Its primary functions are to support the field operations and to represent the sheriff's department on horseback. An added benefit of the posse is to protect the historical heritage of the sheriff and serve as an outstanding public relations tool. (SLOSD.)

The countywide bomb task force consolidates finances and staff in order to create an exceptionally well-equipped explosives unit. Sgt. Jerry Lenthall, from the San Luis Obispo Police Department, is shown above demonstrating the specially designed response truck. Equipped with a robot, explosive entry tool, bomb containment vessel, and satellite communications link, the bomb task force is prepared to respond to all types of bomb- or explosive-related situations. (SLOSD.)

The Sheriff's Underwater Search and Recovery team shares its equipment during a community event in San Luis Obispo. The team uses a blend of sworn deputy sheriffs and civilian volunteers, with Sgt. Andy Rasmussen shown on the right. Sadly, much of the work is centered on the recovery of drowning victims. (SLOSD.)

One of the most dedicated citizen volunteers was Carl E. Lowgren, who was assigned to the training unit. After retirement from a career in the US Navy, Lowgren worked over 10,000 hours during his seven-year tenure, performing duties previously handled by a sworn deputy sheriff. In recognition of his service, the main auditorium used for training was named in honor of Lowgren, who lost his valiant battle with cancer in November 1994.

A huge supporter of community policing, Sheriff Williams initiated a number of programs such as the Sheriff's Auxiliary Volunteer Patrol, designed to assist patrol deputies in each of the communities. The first vehicle dedicated to the SAVP program was donated by Christianson Chevrolet in Arroyo Grande. Pictured above are, from left to right, Mr. Christianson, Sheriff Williams, and Jack Jones, president of the Sheriff's Advisory Council. (SLOSD.)

The Sheriff's Citizens' Academy was implemented by Sheriff Ed Williams to improve the understanding of the working of the sheriff's department as a community-based policing program. Participation in the program was also popular with the sheriff's department civilian personnel. Shown here, from left to right, are Sheriff Williams, Crime Prevention Specialist Terri Woods, and legal clerk (and academy graduate) Albert Calizo. (SLOSD.)

Deputy Sheriff David Marquez demonstrates the proper protocol for detaining a high-risk suspect during the Sheriff's Citizens' Academy. One of the benefits of the citizens' academy is the opportunity to demonstrate and explain the rationale behind the tactics deployed during the enforcement of the law by patrol deputies. (SLOSD.)

As members of the Sheriff's Citizens' Academy look on, Deputies Ray Johnson (left) and Sonja Ott (O'Donohoe) demonstrate a high-risk approach in a vehicle stop. Both deputies were members of the Special Problems Unit, which serves as a street crimes enforcement team concentrating on specific concerns such as drug dealing, registered sex offenders, burglary, and narcotic abuse. (SLOSD.)

Although Sheriff Williams worked normal business hours, he was a frequent attendee of the Citizens' Academy held in the evenings. In this photograph, Sheriff Williams waits with Jim Clark, the Cal-ID coordinator, for students to arrive in the crime laboratory for a tour and presentation. (SLOSD.)

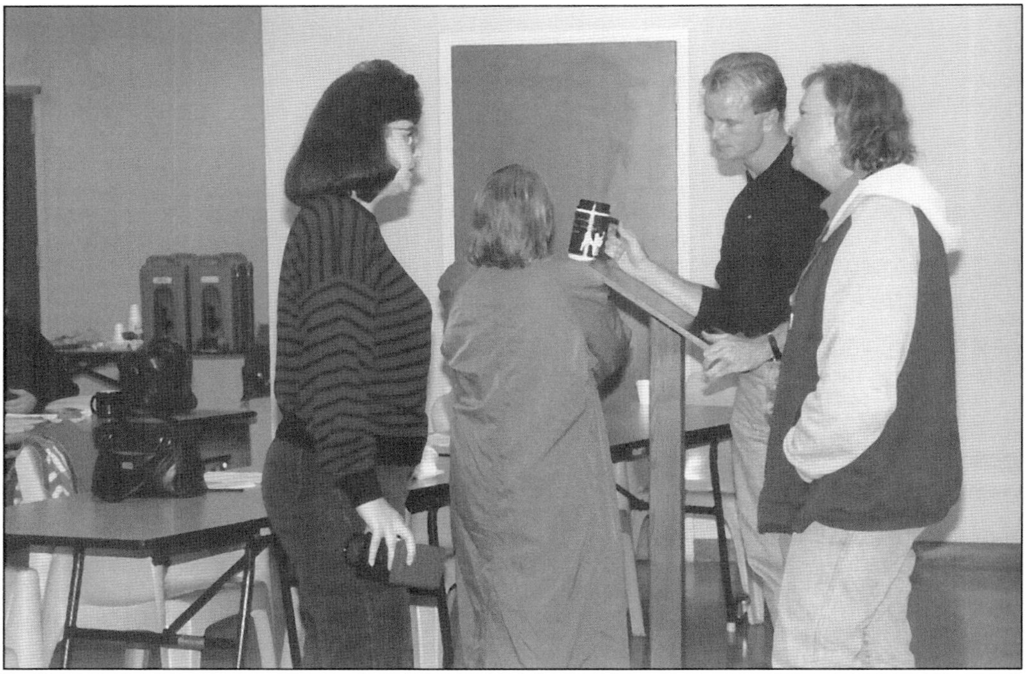

Two of the county's most renowned experts in gang investigations offer a presentation during the Sheriff's Citizens' Academy. Deputy probation officer Loyce Tobler and Deputy Sheriff Justin O'Donohoe gained such insight into gang culture and their families that their expertise was often used in court to establish gang membership and the consequential increase in prison sentence. (SLOSD.)

In an early photograph of the Special Problems Unit and Gang Task Force team members, deputies were freed from handling calls to perform specialized enforcement details to solve problems throughout the county. This c. 1994 photograph includes, from left to right, deputy sheriffs Steve Cruce, Jim Taylor, Nick Fontecchio, and Russ Flores. (SLOSD.)

A makeshift command post was quickly assembled to coordinate a barricaded-subject incident in north Morro Bay on February 20, 1996. This event lasted overnight until the suspect was captured without incident at daybreak. The mobile emergency command vehicle was brought in to the site to support the event under adverse weather conditions. (SLOSD.)

Senior deputy sheriffs Steve Himmelrich and Brad Melson take a quick break from a barricaded subject special enforcement detail call-out in Morro Bay. Operating throughout the night during a rainstorm and in cold weather appears to have no impact on the spirits of these two professionals. Both men had served as team leaders based on their tactical expertise. (SLOSD.)

Staffing of the mobile command vehicle during a barricaded subject call in Morro Bay includes, from left to right, Lt. Greg Buerr of the Morro Bay Police Department, Capt. Gary Hoving, and Chief Deputy Nick Marquart. Such a specially equipped vehicle provides a gathering site safe from the weather and a location for consolidated command by appropriate decision-makers. (SLOSD.)

The camaraderie and respect shared amongst the staff of the sheriff's department is most evident in this photo with Deputies Eric Jackson and Sonja O'Donohoe. The ability to work well with a partner has the potential for becoming a critical factor in survival. Jackson is outfitted with his special enforcement detail uniform and bullet-resistant Kevlar vest. (SLOSD.)

What started as a simple arrest of a parole absconder quickly escalated to a barricaded subject incident in an Oceano mobile home park on February 14, 1996. Deputies Justin O'Donohoe and Paxton Pembroke take cover while setting up a perimeter prior to the arrival of the SED team. (SLOSD.)

Increased mobility and live-feed broadcasting began in the 1990s in San Luis Obispo County, creating an additional burden for incident commanders to control a dangerous situation while providing media access, such as during this Oceano barricaded-subject incident. Camera crews were on scene and televising activities within 30 minutes of hearing of an incident. (SLOSD.)

Rarely issued, the Medal of Valor is the highest award issued for heroism through the San Luis Obispo County Deputy Sheriff's Association. This medal was adopted by the association about 1981 to become the first formalized awards program. It is only issued to a member who serves in a heroic manner above and beyond the normal scope of duties.

Senior dispatcher Trina Strong is working in the County Communications Center, with Sgt. Pete Hodgkin in the background. All 911 and service calls are received and dispatched from a centralized location. The communications center operates within the County Emergency Operation Center, which is the nucleus for all types of emergencies from enforcement activity to natural disasters. (SLOSD.)

Deputy Barney Foster is shown above during a high-risk training demonstration. As a member of the Gang Task Force, Foster performs his specialized operation wearing either a uniform, plainclothes, or modified wear depending on the nature of the particular enforcement objective. Wearing a modified uniform above, he dons a field jacket with identifying insignia, a duty belt, and non-uniform denim pants. (SLOSD.)

The value of forensic evidence as a crime-fighting tool was recognized as early as 1915 by the sheriff's department. Shown above are two specially equipped vehicles for emergency response to crime scenes from the late 1980s. Each unit is outfitted with highly specialized tools and equipment to process practically any type of crime scene. (SLOSD.)

Photographs of most of the elected and appointed sheriffs are displayed on a large framed board inside the lobby of the sheriff's department. Included in the list of those who have served are Henry Dalley, M.C. Rollin Hoyt, Albert Mann, John Lappin, Jacob Schieferli, Francisco Castro, Jose Maria Munoz, Jose Antonio de la Garza, David Norcross, George Mauk, W.J. Oaks, John

Scott, A.C. McLeod, E. F. O'Neal, E.C. Ivins, Yancy McFadden, Charles Younglove, Charles Taylor, Jess Lowery, Walter Carpenter, Harry Haskins, Murray Hathway, Paul Merrick, Lawrence Mansfield, John Pierce, Timothy Storton, George Whiting, Edward Williams, Nicholas Marquart, James (Patrick) Hedges, and Ian Parkinson. (SLOSD.)

A local tribute to fallen officers from around the state is held each May in Mission Plaza, downtown San Luis Obispo. This event is led by Sheriff Ed Williams during the presentation of taps. In the background, officers and deputies stand at attention in respect for peace officers killed in the line of duty. (SLOSD.)

One of the most successful programs developed by Sheriff Williams was the bicycle giveaway program. Williams instructed county jail inmates to repaint and restore hundreds of bicycles each year to give away to underprivileged children. Included with the bicycles are helmets provided by a local bicycling club in an effort to promote safety. (SLOSD.)

Members of the County Bomb Task Force remove boxes of explosive blasting caps found to have been stored in a resident's closet for over 50 years in the Garden Farms area. The explosives were transported in a specially designed bomb container mounted on a trailer to Camp Roberts, where they were disposed of by detonation. (SLOSD.)

Chief Deputy Gregory Slane wears his class-A uniform during a general assembly event at the Sheriff's Honor Farm. Slane retired after a long and successful career concluding his service on the executive team. His son, Gower Slane, joined the department working as a deputy sheriff and carrying on the family tradition in law enforcement. (SLOSD.)

Shown here are Deputy Sheriff Jack Heller and Deputy Sheriff John Black on patrol at Lake Nacimiento aboard one of the sheriff's fleet of watercraft. Annual boat patrol season spans Memorial Day Weekend to Labor Day Weekend to serve the large influx of visitors to area lakes. (SLOSD.)

Senior Deputy Todd Steep patrols the waterways on an inflatable boat, which has been reconditioned from military surplus. This boat is fast and highly maneuverable, serving as an excellent platform for both rescue and enforcement. Deputies patrol the lakes during the summer months and remain available to respond to off-season incidents. (SLOSD.)

Lt. Patrick Hedges ran a successful campaign and was elected sheriff in 1998. Hedges had experience in a variety of assignments throughout the sheriff's department and was well educated for the position. He was reelected twice and served as the sheriff until January 2011.

Upon the early retirement of Sheriff Edward William in August 1998, the likely successor became James Gardiner, the chief of police for the City of San Luis Obispo. Chief Gardiner was highly qualified with many years of executive level leadership experience. During the primary election, Gardiner received 48.2 percent of the vote, with Lieutenant Hedges at 42.2 percent, and Thomas Garrity (formerly a captain) at 9.2 percent.

A newly constructed patrol station was built in Templeton, opening its doors to the public about 2006. The modern facility was large enough to accommodate all of the existing staff, with features permitting expansion upon the growth of personnel projected for the years to come. Project liaison for the construction project was Lt. Rob Reid. (SLOSD.)

A grand opening ceremony and barbecue were held at the new North County Sheriff's Station located on North Main Street in Templeton. This building replaced a series of rented buildings used for patrol operations, moving many times from various locations including Atascadero, Paso Robles, Templeton, and even as cotenants with the California Highway Patrol at the Templeton office. (SLOSD.)

During a presentation at a general assembly, Steve Odom is promoted to sergeant. Shown, from left to right, are Sheriff Hedges, district attorney chief investigator Doug Odom, and newly appointed Sgt. Steve Odom. Doug Odom pins the sergeant badge on his son, Steve, making the ceremony a very special event, and illustrates the many family links in the law enforcement profession. (SLOSD.)

Posing during a brief lull before Mardi Gras enforcement are Deputy Dave Lipanovich, Deputy Doug Scotto, Chief Deputy Gary Hoving, and Deputy Chris Piorotte. The annual ritual has served as a source for widespread damage in the Foothill Boulevard area of San Luis Obispo, adjacent to the Cal Poly State University campus.

The countywide Bomb Task Force members in 2010 include, from left to right, Cathy Bianchi, J.D. Cronin, David Walker, and Robert Eckrote. This team of experts is highly skilled in performing a very dangerous function. Armed with the latest in technology and equipment, the task force is trained by the US Army and the FBI at Redstone Arsenal in Alabama.

A joint training exercise uses a helicopter from the US Customs Service to rapidly deploy members of the Sheriff's Special Enforcement Detail (SED) into a high-risk location. The team trains for virtually any conceivable threat or scenario so as to be prepared for any situation that may present itself in San Luis Obispo County. (SLOSD.)

Training sessions by the SED team are rarely released to the public to protect the confidentiality of their tactics. In this photograph, the team is practicing rapid boarding from boat to boat. The special enforcement detail trains for every potential event to protect the community in the most unusual of circumstances. (SLOSD.)

Target practice from a boat proves to be extremely difficult with the roll and movement of the tide. However, when such a skill is needed to resolve a violent threat occurring upon a waterway, the special enforcement detail will be ready to meet the challenge with lethal precision. (SLOSD.)

Hiring forensic specialist Jones constituted the end of a long-term goal to replace sworn peace officers, who had been conducting crime scene investigations, with highly skilled civilian experts. The civilianization of the laboratory has proven tremendously successful. Shown, from left to right, are Chief Deputy Gary Hoving, Forensic Specialist Kenneth Jones, and Sheriff Hedges. (SLOSD.)

Forensic specialist Jeanine West and volunteer Karen Jones host an educational exhibition during the annual Sheriff's Day at the Ranch. As a forensic specialist, West is responsible for the collection of evidence from crime scenes, examination of evidence, photography, and fingerprint identification as well as a wide variety of scientific examinations. Her function is of critical importance to all major crimes investigations as well as to select coroner investigations throughout the county.

Cal-ID coordinator John Means assists in fingerprinting hundreds of children for personal identification during a Sheriff's Day at the Ranch event. The Cal-ID program is a countywide automated fingerprint documentation and search system linked to state and federal databases. Funding has been approved by a small assessment on fees collected from vehicle registrations.

The Sheriff's Aero Squadron members shown here in December 2010 include, from left to right, Capt. Jens E. Hansen (commander), Allen Andersen, Lt. Michael Cannon, Stephen Frank (seated), Lt. James Ciernia, Lt. Ron Rose, Lt. John Rogers, Abe Viero, David Dickey (past commander), Ronald Blakey, Gene Gailey (past commander,) Lt. Michael Amorteguy, Lt. Bryan DuVall (past commander), Marco Rizzo, James Black, Dr. Robert Harway, Robert Bergman, John Cromwell, and Lonny Rollins.

Always preparing for incidents it hopes will never occur, the Special Enforcement Detail conducts a large-scale training exercise at Hearst Castle, built by William Randolph Hearst. The castle had actually been the location of a terrorist bombing in the early 1970s, damaging one of the guesthouses but only missing visitors by minutes. (SLOSD.)

A changing assessment in the types of potential threats against the nation has changed the level and nature of emergency-response training. In preparation for a weapons-of-mass-destruction scenario, the Special Enforcement Detail raised its response capability by training in heavily protective chemical suits. (SLOSD.)

The California Law Enforcement Historical Society received a seed donation by the San Luis Obispo County Sheriff's Advisory Council to create a traveling museum. Such a cooperative effort between the advisory council and the historical society has served as an excellent model for reaching the community and providing this unique educational tool, which has been viewed by well over 5,000 visitors throughout the state. Crystal Hoving serves as a docent and provides information to Jean Holeman. (Calpolicehistory.com.)

Visitors to the California Police Museum are treated to a variety of exhibits outlining the chronological advances to law enforcement from 1850 to modern times. Included in the galleries are information and artifacts relating to the Gold Rush, Victorian-era policing, the Prohibition period, postwar advancements, and current tools of the trade.

In Memoriam: Charles J. Taylor. On February 26, 1929, Sheriff Charles Taylor was killed in a single-car traffic accident one mile south of Santa Margarita at the top of Cuesta Grade. The sheriff had been returning to San Luis Obispo from an investigation in the Paso Robles area while driving the only car owned by the county. Taylor had been a peace officer since 1907, when he became a member of the San Luis Obispo Police Department. In 1910, he was appointed as a deputy sheriff until he was elected the constable of the San Luis Obispo Township in 1911. He then successfully ran for sheriff and took the oath of office on January 4, 1914. The name of Charles Taylor is engraved in stone at the National Law Enforcement Memorial in Washington, DC, in honor of his death in the line of duty.

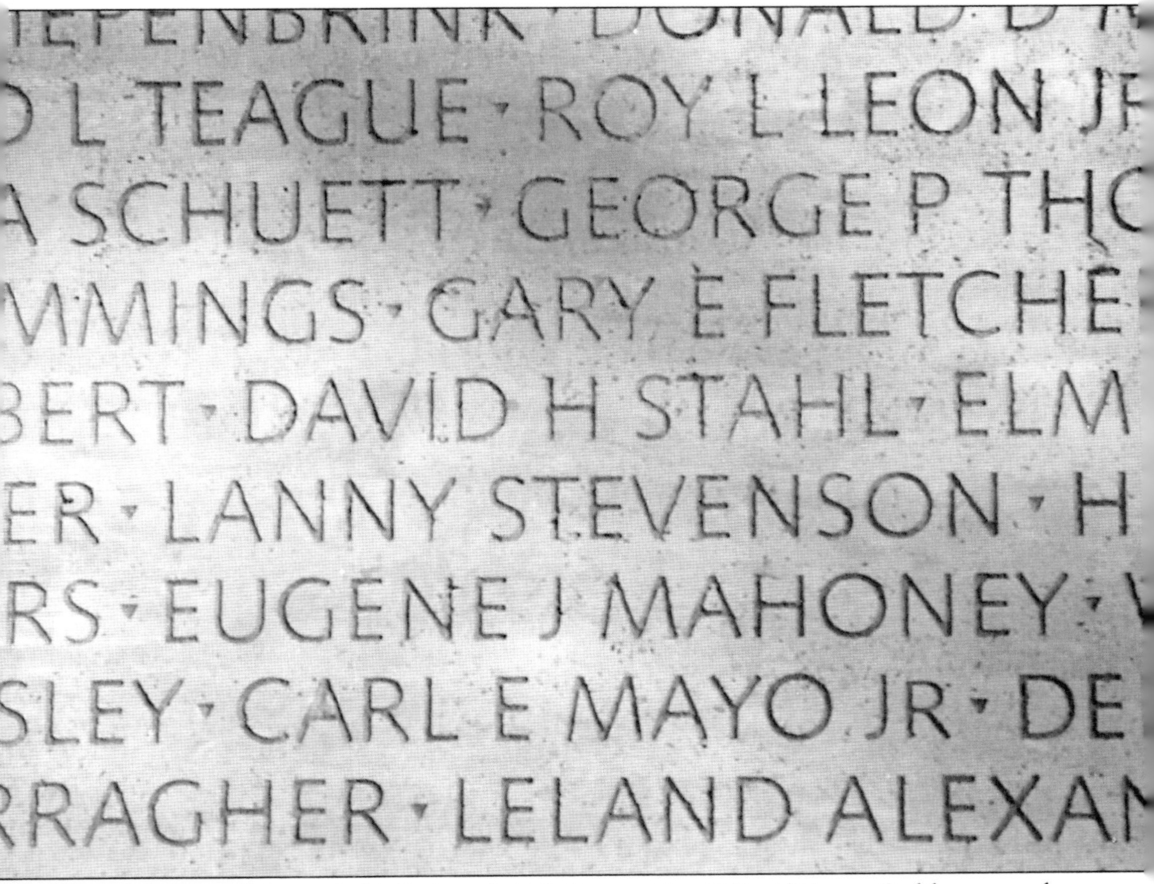

In Memoriam: David Harvey Stahl. On June 9, 1961, Deputy Sheriff David Harvey Stahl attempted to arrest a man suspected of committing a series of crimes, including kidnapping. At about 1:40 p.m. on Old River Road near Atascadero, the suspect was located and confronted. During the arrest attempt, the suspect shot Stahl in the neck and then in the head, inflicting wounds that proved fatal. The tragedy occurred just hours before Deputy Sheriff Stahl was scheduled to attend his daughter's graduation from Paso Robles High School. The suspect was quickly arrested and charged with the murder of Deputy Sheriff Stahl. A jury convicted the suspect, and he was later sentenced to the death penalty. Due to a legal technicality, the suspect was retried, again convicted, and again sentenced to the death penalty. However, in 1966, the California Supreme Court reduced the conviction to second degree murder. The man was released from prison on parole in 1975, and freed from his parole in 1978. The name of David H. Stahl is engraved in stone at the National Law Enforcement Memorial in Washington, DC, in honor of his death in the line of duty.

The badges worn by the San Luis Obispo County Sheriff's Department have primarily been in the shape of a star. On the left is the badge used by each sheriff starting in 1909. Upon the transfer of the badge from the outgoing sheriff to the newly elected sheriff, each man scratched his name or initials on the reverse. The chief deputy badge was in use from about 1920 to 1945.

Undersheriff Harry Needham selected a shield-shaped badge (seen on the left) adorned with his name during a portion of his tenure in the 1930s. The star-shaped badge was issued to Albert Call in 1943 upon acceptance of his appointment as a deputy sheriff. During this era, the department had yet to adopt a consistent style of symbol, resulting in a variety of designs used as the official badge of office.

At left is the undersheriff badge issued to Charles Bowden in the late 1940s. This example represents the design of many badges used through the 1950s and closely resembles the design used by the Los Angeles County Sheriff's Department. The remaining badge was the last one issued to Undersheriff Albert Call, which he was able to keep upon retirement in 1968.

The large six-point star with the California State Seal in the center was issued to full-time deputy sheriffs in the late 1940s and 1950s. The smaller badge on the right was the first department-wide badge, issued from about 1963. Sheriff L.R. Mansfield adopted many changes in policies and uniforms during his tenure.

In 1970, the sheriff's department adopted a larger, seven-point star with the California State Seal in the center. At the same time, the department adopted a new shoulder patch and transitioned from tan to dark green pants while retaining tan shirts. The current badge style was adopted in 1989 by Sheriff Edward Williams. It retains the seven-point shape but includes a custom county seal in the center and uses a dark blue enamel background with gold letters.

The San Luis Obispo County Sheriff's Department has issued only two styles of uniform shoulder patches. On the left is an example of the first issue patch, in use from 1955 through 1970. The current style of patch is a unique shape used since 1970 and illustrated on the right.

Five

A Promising Future

As the first decade of the 21st century comes to a close, America has been thrust into a recession rivaling the Great Depression of the 1930s. Unemployment levels have broken records, county government struggles to balance its budget, and the sheriff's department has realized a reduction in deputies protecting the communities. Performing more with less funding is the new mandate for the sheriff as Patrick Hedges retires from public service.

The November 2, 2010, election resulted in Ian Parkinson emerging as the new sheriff of San Luis Obispo County. His vast experience and popularity were validated by the election results.

Parkinson faces many challenges in leading the members of the sheriff's department into the next era of public safety. Financial effectiveness is likely one of the main goals as he steps into his new role. Following the budget will be the restoration of public trust, which saw a decline in the previous few years. Parkinson's executive style presents an opportunity to provide leadership and quickly earn the respect of the citizens who receive their protection from the sheriff's department.

Finally, the application of technological tools to improve efficiency and effectiveness of personnel is long overdue and a task high on the list for the newly elected sheriff of San Luis Obispo County. While many of the police agencies in the county have been using in-car computers to speed communication, the sheriff's department is still in the test phase for the mobile data terminals.

The sheriff is responsible for managing a budget of $57.2 million with a staff of 377 full-time employees patrolling an area of about 3,200 square miles. In 2010, the salary for the elected sheriff was listed at $182,104 annually.

While the challenges are many, the newly elected sheriff has the opportunity to improve the organization through leadership, technology, and strong management qualities. Such honorable traits are welcome, and the staff of the sheriff's department appear open to the many positive changes expected from Sheriff Parkinson.

Campaign signs adorned the entire county in the closely contested political race for the office of sheriff in 2010. Ian Parkinson adopted a color scheme of green and gold, seen in this image from Nipomo, to attract the eyes of motorists.

Joe Cortez blanketed the communities with large blue signs encouraging voters to support his candidacy for sheriff. Cortez brought a very high level of education and leadership experience as a chief of police to the forum.

Accepting the oath of office by County Clerk Julie Rodewald, Ian Parkinson officially becomes the San Luis Obispo County sheriff-coroner on January 3, 2011. Parkinson waged a hard-fought, two-year campaign for the office, defeating five other candidates. The noon ceremony was witnessed by an overflow crowd of well-wishers in the board of supervisors' chambers in San Luis Obispo.

Upon officially accepting the oath as sheriff-coroner, Ian Parkinson appointed Martin Basti as his undersheriff, who will serve as the second-in-command. Basti had held the position of chief deputy and was one of the most tenured members of the San Luis Obispo County Sheriff's Department. Parkinson (left) pauses for a photograph with Basti only minutes before the swearing-in ceremony.

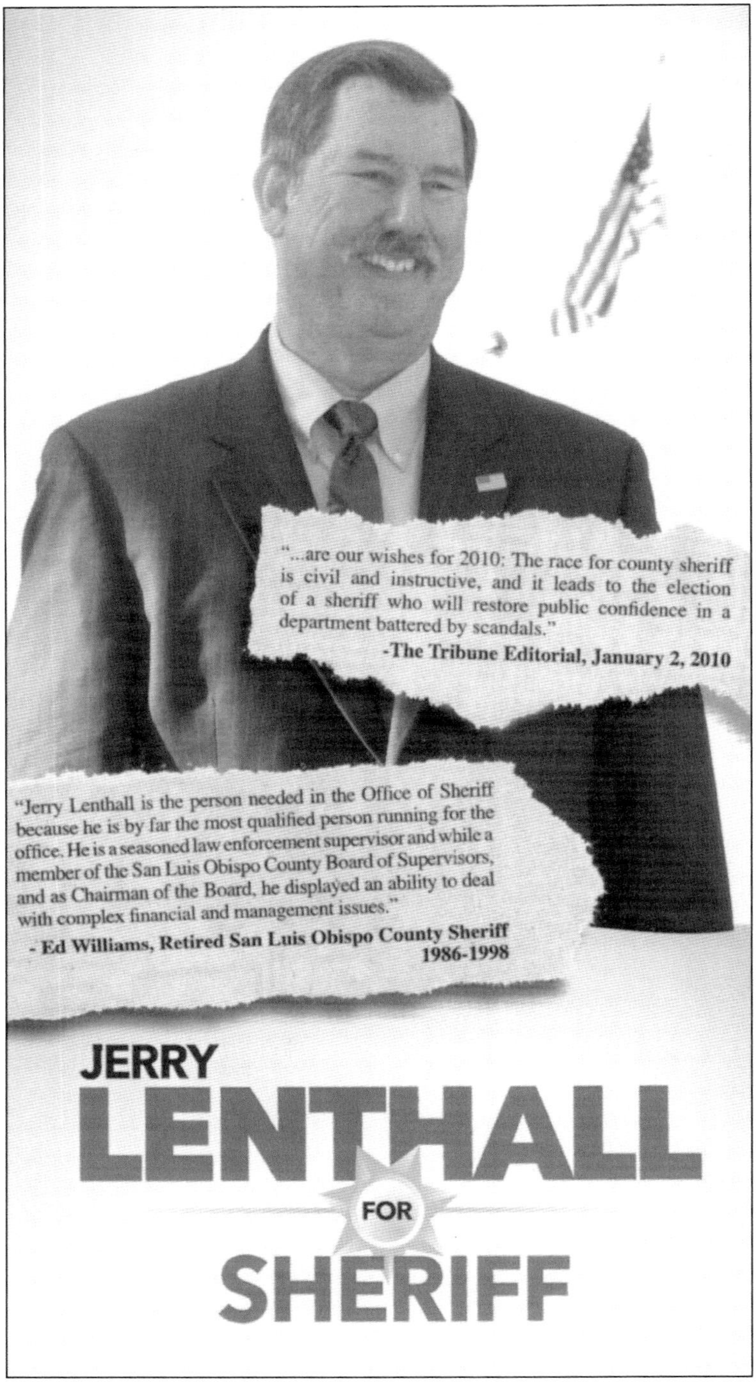

Upon the decision of Sheriff Pat Hedges to retire, the field of candidates for sheriff in 2010 included Jerry Lenthall, Benjamin Hall, Mark Adams, Michael Texiera, Joe Cortez, and Ian Parkinson. The June 8, 2010, primary election results were 41.2 percent for Parkinson, 18.1 percent for Cortez, and 16.5 percent for Lenthall, with the final three candidates accounting for the remainder of the votes. The November general election resulted in Ian Parkinson receiving the highest number of votes for the office of sheriff. He was sworn into office on January 3, 2011, in San Luis Obispo.

The California Law Enforcement Historical Society

Established in 2001, the California Law Enforcement Historical Society is a nonprofit, public-benefit educational corporation with the sole intent of preserving the rich history of peace officers who have served throughout the state of California. The objective is to link those interested in preserving law enforcement heritage and providing a forum for education, research, and the enjoyment of the past. These objectives are met through a website, seminars, collector shows, publications, documentary films, archives, artifact collections, and a museum.

One goal of the society was to construct a traveling police museum for exhibition at a variety of venues throughout California. This goal was realized in 2007 and has been shared with thousands of visitors from Los Angeles to Sacramento. The exhibits within the museum continue to grow and change, thanks to the help of members and other supporters.

The official publication of the society is the *California Police Historian*. Published quarterly, the newsletter contains historical articles, current information about events, membership activities, and other items that may be of interest to the members. Most of the articles and materials are unpublished elsewhere.

Those interested in preserving the history of law enforcement are encouraged to show their support by joining as a member in the California Law Enforcement Historical Society. Further information is available at calpolicehistory.com.